THE DAYS AFTER ALWAYS

THE DAYS AFTER ALWAYS

NEW AND SELECTED POEMS

ANGELA KIRBY

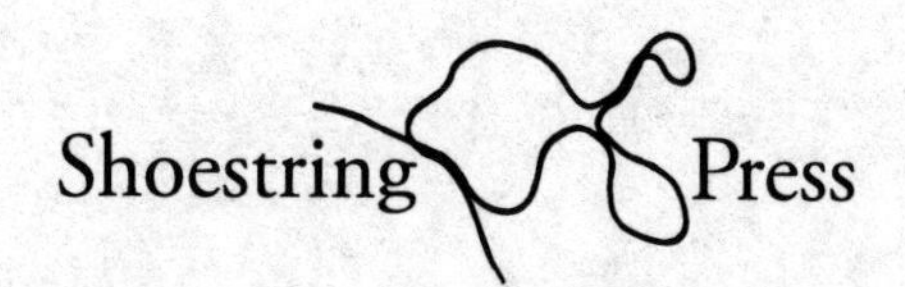

Printed by imprintdigital
Upton Pyne, Exeter
www.imprintdigital.net

Typeset by narrator
www.narrator.me.uk
info@narrator.me.uk
033 022 300 39

Published by Shoestring Press
19 Devonshire Avenue, Beeston, Nottingham, NG9 1BS
(0115) 925 1827
www.shoestringpress.co.uk

First published 2015

ISBN 978-1-910323-38-0

ACKNOWLEDGEMENTS

Acknowledgements are due to the following where many of these poems or earlier version of them have appeared: Agenda, Amaryllis, Ambit, Artemis, Brittle Star, *Requiem*, *Running Before the Wind*, The London Grip, The London Magazine, Writing Women.

Grateful thanks to Peter Abbs, Phil Bowen, Anne-Marie Fyfe and Roddy Lumsden for their inspiration, criticism and support.

For my family, with love and gratitude

CONTENTS

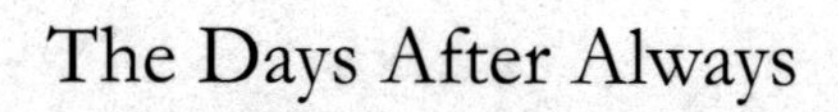

The Days After Always

FOR ALL OF THE FOLLOWING

For my new potato-peeler that hath
delivered me from the mud and scabs
of organic root-vegetables, for this
excellent machine which blendeth
or choppeth all exceeding small, for
my mother's rawhide hat-box
wherein, one day, I may keep a hat
that is not unworthy of it, for my
laptop, spell-check and printer which
now alloweth me to spell 'arrhythmia'
and editors to at least read my poems
before rejecting them, for all those
wondrous skills of an old lover who
waxeth exceeding dextrous with
sailor's knots, also the wisdom of a
new one who expecteth little of me
on his boat, while I forget not our
council for they have erected many
statues in the park, nor the sculptor
who, therein, hath depicted Leda
appearing to strangle a strangely
flaccid swan, for this indeed hath
given me almighty pleasure but above
all for my parents who forgaveth me
much and so too for my children, most
of whom also forgiveth me and who
carryeth me home from pubs and
parties should I begin to sing or dance –
for all these, I praise Thee, Oh Lord
and giveth Thee great thanks.

THE LATE NIGHT CAFÉS OF DESPAIR

I watch them sit alone in the sad archipelagos
of uncleared tables, ketchup bottles, smears
of mustard and brown sauce; stranded there
amongst plates of discarded chicken bones
and lifeless chips, one eye on the door, one
on their watch, waiting for the deceivers
who smile when they lie; for I too have sat
and waited in these places for men like that
waited for them, the uncommitted. Usually
there's a jukebox playing something dead beat
like 'Telstar' and a drunk asleep or arguing
with himself, and almost certainly a bored
waitress reluctant to take my order. In the end
it will be obvious even to me who never learns
or listens that it's one more predictable no-show
and afterwards I'll walk through midnight's
blank-eyed alleys where rats and feral cats
dispute territory between the sleeping bags
of the homeless and spilling dustbins, a cold
wind chasing styrene coffee cups along gutters
back to the emptiness called home, alone there
as my angry father was alone at the end, whisky
glass in hand, helpless and waiting for no-one
adrift in his borderless landscape of the blind.

THE DAYS AFTER ALWAYS

always dough proving in earthenware bowls
beside the iron range, our impatient fingers
betrayed by smudges

always those spirals of sweet grey smoke twisting
up and away from his Navy Cuts

always the evening piano, her voice rising
to us as we try to sleep, when a lovely flame dies
she sings, smoke gets in your eyes

and we are young enough to understand sorrow
and to understand nothing

always waking to dew and distant haymaking
a rattle of milk cans and the mower on the lawn
to days of minnow, dragonfly and wood sorrel

but in the days after always we wake to sirens, sandbags
and refugees, my brother's blood-stained bandages

to Churchill and Lord Haw Haw on the wooden wireless
the announcer's clipped vowels –
Dunkirk, D-Day, Dresden

MEA MAXIMA CULPA

I'm wearing a torn wedding dress
but can't remember the vows. You're
not here, though a man I don't know
is arranging the stiff folds of my skirt
and adjusting a tulle veil so that it falls
over my face. Crows mock from a yew
I scream at them but they shriek back
crowd round me, pecking out flowers
from my bouquet and scattering them
over the earth. I try to pick up the petals
but they turn brown, crumbling to dust
in my fingers. Now someone is laughing
and I'm running down this long path
my hands held over my ears, the gate
seems further and further away, blood
drips down my legs, the white dress
has gone and I'm wearing my father's
best blue shirt which we buried him in.
Reverend Mother has blocked my way,
she and her nuns sing to me in those high
pure voices I hate. *Immaculata, Immaculata*
ora pro nobis, they sing, for they and I know
that everything, as usual, is all my fault.

APPLEWOOD

The Angelus divided my stream-damming
hide and seek hours, doled out time over hedges
cornfields, cottages, over Whitehead's lake
and legless Andrew's dusty ice-cream cabin
sanctifying all the village privies, pigsties
middens and cow pats, celebrated the daily
transubstantiation of my Marmite sandwiches
into the bread of heaven. It chimed without
mercy through all my endless pregnancies
reproached your endless infidelities but now
I watch as the letters of your mistresses
become innocent grey shadows in this bonfire
of sweet slow-burning applewood; they rise
float away over my roses and lilacs, disappear.

LIMOKON

Not one of us remembers when we saw him
for the first time. No, that's not true, we all
remember far too well but what we can't
agree about is where it happened. In one of
those rooms with dim bulbs in parchment
shades, you know the sort, a shop I think
or some kind of bar. He was crouched over
a pile of stuff. Leeks for sure, rice, lambs'
tongues, bay leaves, some kind of fish, pork
fat and a sticky brownish paste labelled *Latik*
though God knows what that was and none
of us speaks Tagalog so we couldn't ask, but
Miranda liked the look of a china dish, one
filled with caramel cream; the man noticed
at once. *Lelang*, he said and patted her hand
Leche flan, very good; she was quite pleased by
that. Later we learnt *Lelang* means Grandma
which was a let down for her, but what I am
trying to get to is what happened next. There
was a sudden cooing sound and a bird flew in,
a dove, I think, with green wings. The man
let out a cry, *Limokon*, and threw a handful
of sesame seeds at its head; then he was gone.
We didn't see him go, but he wasn't there. It
freaked us out, I can tell you. In the end we
put it down to the heat and too much rice wine
at lunch time. After a while we almost forgot
the whole thing and went on with our trip
but then it happened again in another town
another dim lit room and sure enough, another
old man selling odds and sods of weird food.
This time he took my arm, called me *Lelong*
that's right, Grandpa, bloody funny, go on
laugh, why don't you. And the same bird, or
one damned like it, flew in, making the same
cooing noise and *puff*, once again the old guy

wasn't there. You can believe it or not as you wish, I'm merely telling you what happened, that it happened three times more, ask all the others, well, those of us who are left, that is. Miranda's gone, Toby and Lara too, so it's only three of us now, but ask Carol and Jono, they'll tell you all right. What's more, and I give you this for nothing, if a greenish dove should appear and you can hear it cooing, don't hang about.

AT THE IMPERIAL WAR MUSEUM

(formerly Bedlam)

Mr. Softee has parked his van
in the shadow of the great gun
and the Bar-B-Q stall does a brisk trade
in charred meat.

One be-medalled veteran snaps
another who is standing to attention
between the twin barrels.

Inside, beneath the cupola, all is sepia, mud
and duckboards, gangrene, trench mouth
a collage of faded photographs, diaries, letters.

Dear Madam,
I thought you would wish to know as how we found
the Brigadier's horse and are taking care of it…
Jerry was still going for us so we had to leave
Lieutenant Blackshaw and twelve of the lads…

Dear Frank,
Just a note to tell you I went back again this year; not
many of us left now. I was standing next to the old General,
looking at the crosses, miles and miles of them, when he turns
to me and – you won't believe this, Frank – 'What cunts we were,
Sergeant,' he says, nods, put on his hat and marches off.
All the best, Harry.

Children yell, charge headlong over flower-beds
indifferent to the constant rat-a-tat of starlings
and sudden bursts of forsythia along the road
as they dodge the bayonet-spikes of cordylines.

MONTOIS EN RETRAITE

Wind from La Manche cuts though a gap in the dunes, slashes at the hands and face of Montois as he and his battered moped snuffle their arthritic way towards the warmth of the Café de la Paix, evening's refuge from the chill damp of a derelict trailer home squatting in one of Duchamp's sour pastures. He makes for his usual bench under the row of moth-eaten foxes' brushes. Anything that moves in the fields is shot if glimpsed in the hunting season; the wise wear yellow jackets to avoid being taken for deer or boar. He's not a native, Montois, born ten miles away so that to the locals his accent seems queer, though they now accept him, while Jean-Pierre and Nadine look after him well here, knowing that his mother was killed by an Allied bomb during *La Liberation* when he was a child.

He sits quietly, nursing a Calva, watching the crowd at the bar, waiting for Nadine to bring his supper. Tonight he hopes for her special grilled mussels, followed by the best part of a *Tarte Frangipane*, or just maybe one of Jean-Pierre's *tajines*, legacy of service in Algeria, *et puis, poires au vin rouge*. There's music too: young Michel is playing '*J'attendrai*' on a battered sax and this has always been one of Montois' favourites. Often as not he and his moped part company on the way home, both ending up in a ditch where the regulars, who all know the score, find him soon enough and fish him out, cold, wet and whispering *Merci, Je suis desolé.*

HER BEADS

From a lifetime of collecting rosaries
this one with curlicued silver crucifix
and outsize ebony beads was always
her favourite. Now, seeing it hang
unused on a nail beside my bed, I'm
ashamed and full of childhood guilt
for she was seldom seen without it; in
nearly a century, the *Our Fathers*, *Hail*
Marys and *Glory Bes* slipped through
her fingers, easy and sweet as new-
shelled peas, her lips moving silently
as she worked away at the four sets
of Decades, and if the Joyful, Glorious
and Luminous Mysteries were all very
well in their way, she was definitely
far happier with the Sorrowful ones
and indeed when our days grew hard
nothing could cheer her more.

ON ANGLESEY

Certainly Rhosneigr, most probably August
in my mother's hand, *Picnic at the beach! 1928!*
Ten years back from Gallipoli and the Somme,
six uncles lean against Lion Rock, captured
there by a Box Brownie, seemingly at ease, sun
warmed at the sea's edge, Gold Flakes in hand.

Look at them, dapper in white-flannel trousers,
open-necked white shirts, blancoed tennis-shoes,
admire those neat moustaches. If you didn't know
better you might believe those smiles, ignoring
the shadows behind their eyes, the absence of
the youngest brother and that empty sleeve.

IN THE VAL D'ARAN

Sunset, soft airs, below us the village settles
a last eagle planes off on shadowing wings.

You pace the room, caught by another panic attack
and, as if you've sensed it, we hear a far off threat

our room's suffused by light, first pale, then blinding
the night filled with zed-shaped warnings and waves

that overwhelm us. We're trapped, thunder bellows
round us as it ricochets from peak to echoing peak.

Between the flashes, darkness too floods in, so deep
we seem to drown in it. I search for matches, candles

clutch a long-forgotten rosary, try to reassure you
but the valley chalices the storm, offers its black mass

to a no-good god, we two laid out as victims
on fear's altar, praying for deliverance. At midnight

the storm snarls off at last. You sleep, exhausted. I lay
rugs over you, open a window, lean on a wide stone sill

search the now silent sky for hope and Aldebaran
but both remain distant, are light years away.

A BORNEAN HAWK MOTH EXPLAINS

It's the music I make, see, like this, vibrating
my lower abdomen and rubbing my genitals –
it throws them off the scent. Those bloody bats
they're always after us, homing in, insatiable
they are. You can't hear the music? Well, the
bats can, so that's OK, and it buggers up their
sonar; *echolocation*, I think it's called – whatever –
the music does it every time, sends them right
away from me and miles off course. Hell, I may
be just your ordinary small brown hawk moth
but I've got this great trick of flying after them
landing on their balls and laying eggs there
one, two, three, or maybe more, I don't count
excuse me a moment while I rub and vibrate
a little more. Sorry about that; then, as I was
saying, in a while, this is the best bit, one has to
laugh, grubs emerge and munch on the bollocks
which, of course, is the end of those particular
bats' geneaology. Neat, isn't it? But as a matter
of fact, d'you know what, there are some nights
when I could almost feel sorry for them.

EN COTENTIN

Three times three, the Angelus bell is drowning out
the flaunting cockrell in old Mautelain's yard, calling rats
from their tunnels in the straw, freckled Normande cows
to milking sheds and all the oysters of La Manche
to offer up their pearls for well-fingered rosaries. Look
here is Jean-Luc, his tractor's trailer-load of outsize carrots
piled heavenward, pausing to cross himself, more from
habit than from piety, while in the nearby presbytery
M le Curé, keeping time, tups his stout housekeeper
one two, three, one two, three, in the name of the Father.

L'HEURE BLEUE

in this last blue flash of dusk the violins
of our eyes are playing to the south west wind's
counter tenor and the river Seine's low chant

my heart beats a tympany of desire, our music
solves the indigo mystery of twilight and shatters
the drifting cobwebs of the moon spider

the scent I wear sings its own tune of violet
neroli, musk-rose, carnation, bergamot, and look
I leave a diacritic of kisses on your skin

my hand's a bracelet on your wrist, my blood
makes pilgrimage through vein and artery, but you
seem far away, listening to a song that I can't hear

AND TIME PASSES

Psychiatrist tell me it's a syndrome
called *Must clean my tennis shoes*, which
writers suffer from; I've had it all my life.
Some call it time wasting, procrastination
inertia or pure laziness but I prefer to think
of it as seminal meditation, engagement
with that strange synaptic machinery of
the brain, filing away facts, useful or not
(for who's to say?) together with flights
of fancy and vague impressions, all the
while listening to Brahms or The Who
tidying pencils and the button box until
everything churns in the chaotic maw
of a giant kaleidoscope which on some
rare transcendental day may spew out
a rough approximation of a poem
unless at this point it occurs to me that
other chores should take precedence
then while I ruminate on this, all of my
embryonic stanzas escape to waltz off
down the New Kings Road and disappear.
But when I watch how clouds dawdle
across the sky and hummingbirds needle
into the deep hearts of nectared flowers
or indolent fish slip beneath the lily pads
rising occasionally to nipple at the air
it seems to me that the words I want also
arrive like this, wandering for a while, out
of reach, or tongued from the honeyed
daedal depths of thought, finning through
weed's distractions, occasionally making
it to the scrimmy surface of the mind. Then
take my garden, laid out according to every
fine principle of taste; scattered here and
there in seeming artlessness with pretty
conceits: topiary, statuary, knot gardens

terraces, temples, mazes, so like the poet's
fertile brain, don't you think? For weeks
I've planned to sweep it all away, restore
sublime simplicity, could start tomorrow
but first must clean my tennis shoes.

ROSE COTTAGE

(the Morgue, Camp Bastion, Helmand)

All that was left of you was taken there. *Don't worry*
they said *you're safe here, we'll look after you now*

and they cut away the charred shreds of bloodied
combat gear, washed what they could of you, talked

to you, called you by your christian name, then laid
something like our memory of you in a coffin, covered

it with a flag. The plane which brought you home took its
time; we watched it circle down through a slate cloud

the row of unknown Top Brass stood to attention
saluted, a lone bugle carving *Sunset* into the silence.

THE DOWN TRAIN

it is always the same bridge

but this time the crossing is taking longer than usual

while the far side seems much further away   than she'd expected

she knows of course exactly what will be there   the lake naturally

water lilies   a flat bottomed boat, blue paint faded

glints of dragon flies and minnows   a thatched boathouse

half hidden by rhododenrons   while deep in its shadows

is something she does not choose to remember –

so perhaps it might be better to turn back   before too late

even if a black bull   still pounds the earth

in the clover field behind her   raging at her escape

or maybe it is not a bull after all   but the down train coming through

shaking the bridge   snorting out steam as it thunders

below her and besides she's here now   everything lies before her

the ruined folly is just yards away, its door still open   and isn't that the face

of someone she knew long ago   at one of its arched windows?

will the others be there   she wonders, waiting for her

what is it that they want   she would really like to ask them

but the words won't come

THE NIGHT VISITOR

He comes each nightfall. Below my window
ferns part before him, fan-trained plum trees
shiver in their bark, house mice have fled, even
the spiders are hiding. Windows won't save
me, I know that; glass is no match for him.
He will climb the drainpipe, pierce through
the curtains and find me, even though I pull
the eiderdown over my head. Lean, insatiable
implacable hunter, all my life he's followed
me on silent feet, claws sheathed, yellow eyes
cruel slits in the darkness, stained teeth glinting
in shafts of moonlight, his gnarly breath rank.
Blessed candles and Holy Water do not deter
him, my rosary fails me, the red light which
burns before the Sacred Heart is all that stands
between us. Jesus, Mary and Joseph comfort me
oh souls in Purgatory intercede for me, forget
me not in my hour of need; this is a time for
miracles,. Turn my oppressor into ghee, let him
melt back into that malignant jungle he comes
from, Guardian Angel set me free of him after
all these years, oh let my nights be dreamless.

CHITTY MOLL AT THE PINK SANDWICH

Sundays, Chitty Moll gets up late, skips breakfast
snacks on scotch eggs and Battenburg slices
washed down with Emva Cream; same things each
week, why change a winning combo? Sometimes
she thinks of dusting or emptying an ashtray
but that soon passes. No time to waste, life's too
short, days nip by, she has more important
things to worry over, such as what to wear
tonight; black for sure, fringed of course, with
here and there touches of colour: a belt, scarf
shawl, strings of jade or turquoise, perhaps a
turban, sequined headband or long earrings.

That decided, she takes a nap, drifts off, dreams
of Basil Rathbone, Peter Lorre, Bella Lugosi
gurning in her sleep. Ten o'clock sharp; up
dressed, curlers out, boots laced, she's away
bracelets chiming. Four knocks, three rings
the door opens. Bang Bang's there, the Twins
Pretty Pauley and Big Tommo, half listening
as Pikey Joe plays 'Baker Street', switching
to 'Petite Fleur' when Chitty Moll rolls in
nods at the regulars, heads for her usual seat
works away at a plate of pickled eggs and onions
three pints of Guinness and, lingering over a
fourth, tells herself 'Easy gel, best stick to ciggies'.
She inhales, relaxes, waits for the contenders.

A SONG, A SMILE, A SILLY WALK

I say, I say, I say… Last week it was the Met
in the Edgeware Road and now we're queuing
for tonight's big names at the Chelsea Palace, Ed tells me
'You'll adore it, darling '… Archibald, certainly not…

Rob's booked a Box for us and Meredith, we're in…
it's the Two Pirates on first, brawny men
in short frilly skirts, saggy boots, jaunty black hats
with skull and crossbones. After a load of foolery
the little pirate takes a run, right up the body of
big one, balances improbably, fingertips
to fingertips, feet high up behind him in the air
the wire clearly visible. He looks us in the eye
Oh no there isn't… Oh yes there is…

Dee-dum, dee-dum, dummy-dummy dum… there's
sand on the stage ready for the next 'spesh' act
the orchestra slinks into Luigini's 'Egyptian Ballet'
two emaciated and mustachioed men lope on
followed by Betty (except it's Patsy, Betty Knox's'
daughter but we don't know that yet). She's wearing
fringes, tassels and sequins; the whistling starts
as she undulates through 'Cleopatra's Nightmare'
which Mussolini loved while Goebbels ranted
Sie sind untergruben die Moral von Nazi Jugend…

And then they're into the Sand Dance, the audience
goes wild, popping their heads to and fro, poking
flat hands back and forward, Rob gets me smack
in the eye, Ooh, pardon me, young man, I'll trouble yer
to keep yer 'ands to yerself…

At last, it's the Prime Minister of Mirth, the Star Act
George Robey; desist, kindly temper your hilarity with
a modicum of reserve… he gives a few twirls of the cane
a lift of giant eyebrows, raises the top hat – it's behind

you… then he's away – if you were the only girl in
the world and I were the only boy – the House roars back
nuffin' else would matter in the world terday…

then, Goodnight Sweetheart, it's over, the Stars leave
in chauffeur-driven cars, minor acts take buses, back to
claggy digs in Balham or *scarper the letti*, while
Ed, Rob and I make our way home, dancing on the
pavements, singing The Boy I Love is Up in the Gallery.

Sixty years on, Ed and Rob are long gone, I don't
dance down pavements anymore but on YouTube
Wilson, Keppel and Betty are still capering
over the sand and someone somewhere is singing
a little of what yer fancy does yer good.

AT THE ALLE GUGLIE

It rains, a soggy vaporetto
drops us off at a wrong stop
you have taken against the hotel
and lie sulking on the bed.
Let's cancel Venice, you say –
but I say I've waited all
my life for Venice, Buster,
no-one, believe me, cancels it
for me now. Already, despite
the mosquitos, I'm besotted
with it all – the street, our
room, the gilded ceiling
bulging Putti, flaking paint
and the way the chandelier
shakes its red glass beads
in time as lovers in the room
above get down to it.

And still it pours, but now
beneath our window the market
and the tide are in full flood
women in yellow gumboots
argue the toss over the high price
of aubergines and even you
beloved, cannot resist for long –
we sally out to strut our stuff
on swaying duckboards
wobbling like tyro acrobats
arms outstretched, waving
our red umbrellas.

There before us, all Venice lies –
her sights, smells and gondolas
scenes by Canaletto, risotto nero
in that trattoria by the Bridge
of Sighs, these over-priced Old-
Fashioneds, knocked back
in Harry's Bar and at last, after
three of these, you've grown
mellow, mellow, mellow.

BLAME IT ON THE RAIN

April outdid itself, those ever-longer days
lightening to lilac, birdsong, the early roses
and moreover you were there. For the first
few days we plotted summer with all those
places that we planned to see. Maybe the
Shetland Isles or Sicily in August? Some old
friends, the odd cathedral, standing stones
perhaps five days in NYC and better still
two weeks in our longed for sanctuary, just
off the coast of Maine? But then, it rained
you haven't forgotten that? Not fleeting
light-fingered *arpeggios* but a non-stop roll
troppo and *rallentando* on our roof. Looking
back on it now I see how that was pretty
much the way things went on afterwards
alternate highs and lows, though we didn't
see it at the time. Good days which one of
us would spoil; me with sarcasm and my
dodgy map-reading; you with occasional
sweetness followed by a sudden rage, or
your laid back incompetence with the car
but none of that so different from before.
Can all of this be only six short years ago?
Some nights I wonder how you are.

HEADING TO ISLE AU HAUT

We're just half-way at Jo-Jo's diner
where her red-haired help makes
out to frisk us, in case, as she says
we have pocketed all her fresh
dough-balls, then, on cue, calls
after us, 'have a nice day now'
and playing native, like we're
the couple before us in the blue
Winnebago, 'plannin' to', we say
as I pull out back on the road
while from the radio, Janis belts
out 'Bobby Magee', which seems
somehow like a sort of sign
that maybe things will be OK
now, after our sticky dawn-start
from a dud motel, somewhere
near Prout's Neck, but that was
then; afterwards there were more
wrong turnings and in the end
we never did get there, we never
quite made it to Isle-au-Haut.

HELLEBORES

At night, she dreams of him
his wan and freckled face
the day he went away
to school. She cups it
in her hands, turns it up
to hers, kisses it. When
she wakes, his name is on
her lips. *Bran*, she whispers
Bran, my little bran-face.
Later, in the garden
kneeling by a shaded bed
beneath the lilac trees
she runs her fingers through
the soil, keeping it friable.
Leaves push up in spring
the waiting gets harder, at
last the flowers-heads come.
She turns their wan and
freckled faces upwards
chooses seven, places them
in the silver vase she keeps
beside his photograph
and six framed medals.

IN THE 5TH ARRONDISSEMENT, 1949

'here is good broken music' Troilus and Cressida, iii.1.

The girl who has never been loved leans out
from a third-floor window in La Rue des Ecoles.

In the room behind her, Henri Salvador sings
from a wind-up gramophone on a Polydor 78.

Maladie d'amour, he sings, *maladie de la jeunesse* –
and the girl weeps, her tears falling on couples

who crowd the street below. It is April, in Paris
a cliché for which I apologise, forgive me, but this

is how the story goes. April, the 5th arrondissement
with its cafés, their striped awnings floating out

beneath the chestnut trees which are in bloom.
Merde alors, two more clichés. The girl who has

never been loved turns back to the room, puts on
another record. Henri sings only for me, she thinks

and sings with him; together now they make their
broken music. *Il y a bien longtemps, bien longtemps que*

J' l'attends, they sing, *Alors je lui dis: Pourquoi t'es partie?*
Pourquoi t'es partie? All my life, she thinks, all that my life

has been is broken music. I'm nineteen, far from Les
Sables d'Olonne, hollow for love in a city of lovers.

MASH

It drove her wild, the way he took over the stove
when there she was, trying to get dinner on the table

with what was left of the rations, any old bits
and pieces she could lay her hands on, slices of rabbit

between layers of sage-and-onion forcemeat
Poor Man's Duck, she called that one, or perhaps a pie

of curried root-vegetables, from a stained recipe
in one of those leaflets sent out by the Ministry

but whatever it was, he would always ruin it
with his heavy iron pan of stinking hen food

though what really got to her was his timing
and the performance he made as he stood there

beetroot-faced and sweating, bent over the mash as
if, she said, he was winning the war single-handed

him with his cabbage leaves, potato peel and bacon rinds
together with the scraps he tipped from our plates

before we'd half-way finished with them, and then
on top of it, he'd make out he was doing it for us.

How did we think he kept the family in eggs, plus
a capon most Sundays, and now there we were

the ungrateful lot of us, sidling out of the kitchen
fingers held to our noses, away from the steam

the smell and their angry voices, off to the Anderson
gas masks in hand, pulling blankets over our ears.

MINISTERS OF GRACE

It's a night of black rain
lancing headlights, blurred haloes
a thousand saints hover
over the motorway, I catch glimpses
of Kenelm, Fabiola and Petroc
angelic advance-guards fly wrong-way
up the southbound lanes
towards me, hurling spears
from which neither windscreen-
wipers nor anti-glare shades save me
the Skoda slews out of control
choirs of Seraphim land on the roof
Uriel grabs the wheel, the car takes
off with Tarshish, Metatron and Seraphael
laughing and swearing, swerving
down A-roads, B-roads and back lanes
Raziel and Zophiel whooping it up
alongside. I dive into the back, shut
my eyes, clutch maps, sat-nav
and I-Phone, sing *Dies Irae, dies illa*
pray. At last I gain courage, look out
onto a swirl of wings. Thrones, Powers
Virtues and Dominions throng
about me as a landscape of downs
hedgerows and white cliffs
drops away. As we swing out
across the channel, I change my tune
and jumping out of the car
into the enveloping, irresistible blue
of space, into the arms of Nisroch
Amiel, Phaleg and all that holy crew
I'm yelling *Alleluia, Alleluia, Alleluia.*

PICCADILLY PARADE

Mick and Mike trawl the street, dented toppers
cock a hoop with a pheasant's tail feathers. Mike
pushes the hurdy gurdy, Mick turns the handle
we quickstep round them to its whining roar, the
last rose of summer lies tangled in my hair, it's
still a long way to Tipperary, the nightingales in
Berkeley Square sing *Watch out, watch out, there's
a liar about*, the boy beside me has a dark blue cape
with red silk lining, maybe this is love, morning's
milkmen and dustmen join in, we foxtrot past the
Ritz, Fortnum's, Swan & Edgar, Eros eggs us on.
Milk bottles clatter, dustbins clang out a fast beat
for our carefree feet till night flies up and away
as watches and Remingtons call us to bleak offices
where the young men in Old School ties claim to
know what life is about, we girls almost believe
them, our pens at the ready as we struggle over
Pitmans and Roneo machines till half-past five
when we ride buses back to flats in Kensington
to gas rings, baked beans, Floris-scented baths
stiff taffeta petticoats under strapless dresses
waiting to be taken out for dinner at Quo Vadis
waiting again till the Carousel opens and there
sits pretty Bobby, plump hands on the ivory keys
kiss kiss, playing our specials for each of us, and
it's 'Makin' Whoopee' for me, 'Easter Parade' for
Tony, 'Zing go the Strings of my Heart' for lovely
long-dead Sally. But now our tulle dresses moulder
in forgotten trunks, billowing no longer; the half
remembered boy in a dark blue cloak left long ago
and only the Moët sings in the hollow stems of brittle
glasses, bubbles dancing to a leatherette Dansette.

THE TREASON OF THE CLOCKS

Despite ten inherited brass carriage clocks
and her bedside radio's meticulous precision
with the hours she has lost all track of time
but now clings desperately to its disappearing
shirttails. Is it dawn or dusk? For how is she
supposed to tell? The sky is grey and will not
commit itself nor reveal anything of consequence
yet not so long ago she was at ease with time,
night regularly followed day, the kitchen clock
chimed every quarter, alarms rang as bidden
the gong was firm about lunch, her fake Rolex
and blue Swatch ticked compulsively, the cuckoo
could always be relied on. But today a voice in
her one good ear sings *Baby, Baby, Baby, you're
out of time*, and a man she feels she really should
know walks towards her, smiling, reaches out
says they have a long standing appointment.

ROAD SHOW

When it came to our town the Mayor declared a holiday
not a stroke of work got done, my father blamed the fly-posters

for overnight they had plied their trade and the place got plastered
walls bawling out *Sensational! Educational! Do not miss this!*

the weather was fine – we queued for hours, train drivers left
their engines steaming, road sweepers threw away their brooms

dreaming salesmen abandoned their cars, in St. Opportune's Primary
class-rooms were empty, the dairy closed, milk went sour

the bakery shut, not a loaf of bread to be had, midwives struck
so Mrs.Bucktrout was out of luck and delivered herself

of mewling twins – but eight minutes after she lined them up with
the rest of us, no priority asked, none given; a one-eyed busker

and the ice-cream man both made a fortune, gangs of pick-pockets
had it easy, even kids grabbed a bob or two hawking lemonade

and ginger bangs at tuppence a go, that incredible, indelible day
of the Great Black Whale Road Show, and when our turn came

we filed in through the ebony ribs into a far, high arch of vertebrae –
it haunted us for years – gibbering candles, that sour wet smell

of rot and nightmares – and everything pickled in tar, from
its monstrous, mummified head to the rigid flick of its tail.

WINTER APPOINTMENT

Winter is well advanced, her days drawn in
leaves blackening beneath the frost, trees
pared down to bone and wrinkled skin. You
put out crusts for ruffled birds, throw rinds
say that should keep them through till spring.

It takes two sticks for you to cross the path
to skirt the ice-blind hollows in worn stone
afraid of falling, broken hips. It would kill me
to die in hospital, you say, then laugh, aware
that bread alone will not keep you till spring.

THE RIVERS RUN

death is lilac, hawthorn, lilies of the valley, white roses
death is larkrise, the thrush's song, the cuckoo's call

The Ribble, the Hodder, the Darwin and the Lune flow on
their grey green eddies pulsing through my veins

My mother is saying *green thoughts won't make a garden*, May
air drowsy with privet, elderflower, echoes of her scent.

I fold away her clothes, finger her pearls, her wedding ring
the blue green tourmalines now twisting on my finger.

After six hours weeding, I walk alone through evening lanes
thinking of the boy killed far away early one day in May

but now lying safe under a froth of cow parsley in a village
churchyard where the green oaks stand sentinel for him.

They die in May, the ones I love, my mother, sister, lover, child
I call to them, plead with them *talk to me*, beg them *wait for me* –

death is lilac, hawthorn, lilies of the valley, white roses
death is larkrise, the thrush's song, the cuckoo's call

The Ribble, the Hodder, the Darwin and the Lune flow on
the years grind slowly by, my grief still green, still green.

THE GALOSHES OF MADAME DUJARDIN

They still hang as she last left them on a nail
beside the garden door; her apron, its daisies
wilting now, droops from its accustomed
hook in the kitchen where the shadow of her
long round-bellied clock ghosts the wall beside
this blue dresser while we fancy sometimes
that Felicette, her pet white goat, still bleats
from the outhouse where our logs are stored.
What would they make of it all, old Monsieur
and Madame Dujardin, the ways we've changed
their house, their garden? These roses climbing
walls and into apple trees, a dusky lavender
hedge, this sprawling rosemary? Would our
shower, two bathrooms and new cooker meet
with their approval? We hope they might be
pleased we've kept the rhubarb bed, elder tree
and clump of green-tongued sorrel, the wide
mouthed Normande cheminèe, that black cave
of the bread oven, and by the door this plaster
head of a ruddy-faced sou'westered fisherman
above a rack on which they hung storm lanterns
and great iron keys as our neat Chubbs hang now.

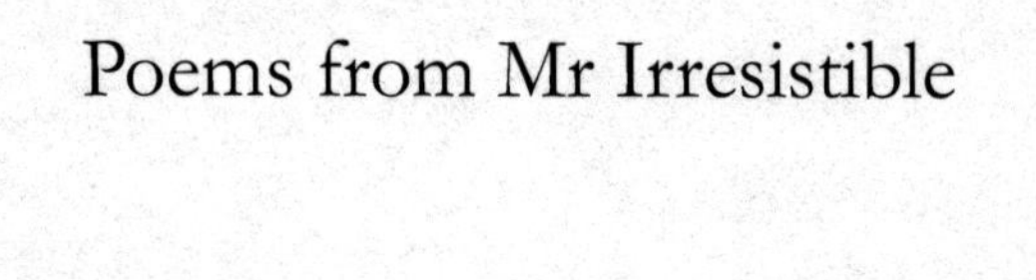

Poems from Mr Irresistible

THE PTILINORHYCHIDAE AND I

This is how the bower-birds live, the Ptilinorhynchidae
and I. According to Britannica we are a link

between the birds-of-paradise and the crows. God knows
we move to strange forces; something inside us clicks

ticks, whirs, stirs; soft cogs turn, our bodies churn
obediently to the red machines which drive us

faster, faster. The collections grow, we do not question,
it is enough to know that anything blue will do

for Ptilinorhynchus violaceous and me; just see
how we lay out our runs and avenues (one yard long,

eight inches wide, see Britannica) with stones, shells
and bleached bones, usually those of the kangaroo

for we are the rare, the very few, we Avians who
use tools and are credited with an aesthetic sense.

The Chlamydera nuchalis and I, we choose to build
our bizarre arbours in thickets of dense shade, come

oh come inside, spend sweet hours with us, share our ways
our hidden ardours. Artists, poets, birds, we take what we must,

tinsel, feathers, glass; crush berries, grass, and mix them
with dust, saliva and our dreams then make a brush

of leaves and fibrous stuff to paint our plaited bowers
with frescoes, as Britannica says. For hours and days

the wild collages grow and glow, sprout silver flowers
under the tide of our desires, the urgency of our beaks.

Come inside, come inside… who seeks to know
and understand us? Who longs to creep deep, deep

into the hearts of the rare bower-birds? Blackfellow
and the Tjurunga stones could show the way, but hurry…

APPLE

Consider the demotic apple
and its black seeds which just now
I spat out into my hand –

grown here in this city garden
where ivy clasps a lichened tree
of unknown lineage, it has

nevertheless, and despite the scab,
all the desired colour, taste and texture
of an apple to commend it –

and see how, in my palm, the future
lies, centuries of jellies, crumbles, pasties,
aeons of *tartes tatin*, charlottes, pies –

here is a millennium of orchards, ice
floes of blossom, a grumbling avalanche
of windfalls, a distant thrum of wasps.

TECHNICOLOUR SUNSET

Streaked with custard
and bottled plum juice, the sun
slurps westward into a Disney sky,
that outrageous cocktail
of sea-greens, blues and violet,
spiked by one sugary star

The cue, of course, is for Snow-white,
with her gaggle of cute dwarfs,
to troll on, merry as all get-out,
swinging lanterns
and trouping their purple silhouettes
across this humpbacked bridge

but the boy sprawled here at my feet,
flopped, flaccid as Dopey
under the streetlights,
in a tangle of leather
and blood-spangled chrome,
has Hi-Hoed off to another place
and will not be coming back.

THE GREY HAIRED WOMAN DEADHEADS HER ROSES

I am afraid in the streets,
they are too full, crowded with feral girls.
Sinuous, otter-sleek, they brush past me,
the breath slipping, sweet as alyssum,
between their small, cruel teeth.

I see them dance and sway
down pavements, gutters, watch
their sapling spines spin to a morning wind,
hear them sing their harsh new words
to my old music.

I am wounded, cut deep
by the sharpness of their eyes.
Such girls, I imagine them turned soft,
turned smooth, twisting supple as green vines
round the hard thighs of their lovers.

Safe here in my garden,
drained of colour by the recent drought,
I watch them pass,
rake the dust a little
and tear the heads from dying roses.

ECHINUS ESCULENTUS

Once you've found them
in the right sort of place,
like this one, for instance,
clear shallowish water
and rocks far enough from shore
to escape the worst of the shit,
everything hangs on the knife,
nine inches or so will do, light
and as sharp as you can whet it,
you don't want to mess about,
not under water, not for long,
not with these little fuckers,
and I'd wear tough gloves
plus some kind of shoe
though not everyone bothers,
while you'll need something,
a bucket or a bag, to drop them in,
and it's best to anchor off,
these outcrops are vicious,
then swim the last few yards,
here we are – dive, slash, grab
and back to the boat, don't
muck around, slice them in half
and eat them at once,
no salt but just as they are
like soft boiled eggs,
all you need is a teaspoon,
look, forget the spikes, try one –
there, now you can see
why they remind me of you –
difficult but worth it.

RICE DREAMS

Who can tell how things are?
Who can be sure, can you?
Last night for instance –
had *you* been in Battersea
at the Golden Elephant
you might have seen
the couple at the corner table
sharing fragrant rice
from a blue-green bowl,
seen him feed her
with translucent shreds
of sticky sweet vegetables,
with those fat prawns
that curl like rosy foetuses
in the hot green sauce
and you might have thought
how charming it all seemed but
suppose the women was his wife
reluctantly playing
a role he had forced upon her,
that for a few hours
she must become for him
the child whose time he'd bought
on his last trip to Bangkok –
what was she, ten, eleven
twelve? – little Mau
who kneels to wash his feet,
the well trained kitten-cat girl
pad-padding up and down his spine,
whose clever small hands
rub and knead him –
Mau, Mau – in his dreams
he calls out for her still
so what, you might ask,
is the wife doing here,
playing these games,

how does she put up with it,
why does she stay?
Fair enough questions I'll admit,
but do not expect any answers.
Life is never that simple,
especially for a wife,
or haven't you noticed?

MR PANUTKA'S FINEST HOUR

Mr. Panutka purses his mouth
and, after some thought,
moves two pins
an infinitesimal distance
somewhere to the south
of a left shoulder-blade
as, on tiptoe, he circles
the general and head on one side
runs his eyes, knowing as a starling's,
across collar, vents, buttonholes,
lapels, appraising the miracle,
this cut of the cloth, this way
he has persuaded it to hang,
mercifully by-passing
that which the general
still thinks of as his waist
and this is Mr. Panutka's finest hour,
this, he realises now,
is what he was born for –
to measure, cut and fit,
to tack and sew these fragile threads
to-and-fro across his President's
dress uniform in which,
very soon, though Mr. Panutka
does not yet know this,
General Ramon Garcia Ramirez
will be shot, at ten o'clock exactly
on the morning of June the fifth,
by one of the mothers
whose sons he tortured
and, smiling over his coffee,
fed to the flesh-eaters
in his shimmering lily pool.

BLACK ICE

Frost has caught the wax hips on the rose.
Beyond the glaucous ranks of cabbages
leaves flare and flicker on the cherry tree.
I loved this garden – she says it quietly
and the past tense throws me. New images
obliterate the old, her painting glows

red, blue and gold, such bold colours
for this last of her interior landscapes,
but now she dreams of crows, foetuses
and snakes. Beside her bed my autumn crocuses
droop on their etiolated stems, fat grapes
reproach and Our Lady of the Seven Dolours

smiles down on us, last relic of lost faith
when we both delighted in the odder Virgins.
Look at my hair, it's starting to fall out,
she says. I hold her tight and blindly tout
faith-healing, nature-cures, the light begins
to go, we talk of everything but death.

BRAIN CORAL

She is not sure about things
any more, or why she is here –
all day long she falls
through the holes in her head
into nowhere, forgetting
her house and her garden.

There, her gloves, trowel,
secateurs and galoshes
wait for her where she left them
in the potting shed,
her terrace is clotted with thyme,
Reine des Violettes
arches over the walls,
the ammonites in the rockery
curl and spiral inward,
everything is as she planned.

At the visiting hour
he brings in a posy
of wild roses and cow-parsley,
tells her that the swallows
are flying lower than usual,
that the death's head hawk-moth
has not yet been seen
and that the wood-pigeons
call to him, as always,
it's your fault,
don't you know?

The brain coral they found
on their last holiday together
keeps the door propped open.

DAVID

Watching you die your high-tech death
is not proving easy though everything
here, this half-world of intensive care,
is antiseptic, efficient, kind, I'll give them
that, but it is not as you wanted, planned,
not the way anyone, any body, would
wish to go, hooked-up to tubes and
monitors, to intravenous drips, and,
watching that hypnotic point of light,
that deranged ping-pong ball, skittering
its way across the screen, watching your
face that is not-your-face turn grey to
fool me that you've already gone,
watching you, stripped and vulnerable,
your body so disturbingly alive, your
brown arms warm, your resilient chest
rising and falling still between these
juddering halts, my heart stops too –
till yours starts up again and, this is
the worst of it, from time to time you
jerk upright, open your eyes to glare
at me – the nurses swear it's just a reflex
but the look is too familiar, so brother,
forgive me, for I *will* mourn you later,
all that I want right now for both of us
is to be out of here and away.

AN AFTERTASTE OF SALT

Men, they never know what they want,
at first they can't get enough of us,
our phosphorescent breasts,
the way our bodies flicker in the dark,
the sequinned flick of our tails,
that risky, salt-aftertaste of anchovies
and seaweed, and us being always
a little ahead of them somewhere,
way out beyond their bowsprits.

They swear then we'll be mistress
of their hearts, queen of their hearth
and home, no jewel too rare for us,
we shall toil not, neither shall we spin
and occasionally we believe them,
tell ourselves it might be worth a shot.

But once they have us ashore,
when the shine and novelty wear off,
they don't know what to make of us,
stay out late or stare into the fire,
take to drink, ignore us, wish
they had thrown us back
while the women cross themselves,
draw in their skirts, walk
on the other side of the road
and teach the children to catcall,
to jeer that we smell of fish.

REMEDIAL ACTION

It took her weeks, months,
to make the appointment
but when she saw him at last
to ask if he could, perhaps,
do something, anything,
about her breasts,
he nodded and cupped them
in his hands so tenderly
that her eyes filled with tears
and, half in love with him,
she listened as he warned her
that all surgery had its dangers,
and might in this case
cause her the loss
of sensation in the nipples,
which made her yearn to tell him
that nipple-sensation was,
like orgasm, a gift she'd never had
though often longed for
but then she remembered –
how once, just once, suckling
her last child, she had felt,
hadn't she? a sweet, slow pull,
an ecstatic tugging that seemed
to run from breast to womb.

FLOATING ISLANDS

separate six eggs… a small blizzard of blossom
frosts the terrace; the cat unknots himself
to go hunting, … 'it's not FAIR'… a diacritic of grief
rises in Gregorian notation from the tree-house
where the ash weeps above contorted limbs

bring milk and sugar to a slow boil… the sun
moves away, the room darkens, shrinks,
and the white grit on her hands turns salt, slithers
into open wounds. 'Mummee… Mummee…'
the cat returns and twitches into sleep

whisk egg-whites… she ladles up small clouds, drops them
into simmering water, watches them sink
and rise again, looks into the mirror of the misted spoon,
sees how, in another room, another place, the sun
shines warmly still. Her clock whirs out 'alone'

return the mixture to the pan and thicken slowly…
the garden encroaches, ivy has broken through
behind the window frame, turned pale; there are ants
in the sugar, the navigation of snails is charted on the tiles
and a brown fist of dead roses beats upon her door

pour into a bowl and chill… all summer long
there were whispers, rustlings, but she would not listen,
could not watch as the polygonum, green stranger, thrust
into the house, climbed the hollow stack and burst
from the chimney, masking triumph with a white veil of petals.

float meringues on the chilled sauce… she calls
the children in, watches as they settle fretfully, elbowing
space at the scrubbed table. She bides her time,
practises her arts, her telarian skills, reweaves
the web, imposes form on disintegration

serve with wild strawberries… at the epicentre,
she ladles six plates with calm cream seas,
scatters puffed-up fancies with offshore fruit.
Look, she says, floating islands,
and wreathes her plate with applemint.

UNPACKING THE SHAWL

It had always been too heavy, she thought,
bumping it down the stairs from the attic

towards the bonfire. Now, its rawhide cracked,
liver-spotted with age and torn labels

under forty years of dust, the brass catches
were corroded and proved difficult to force.

Yesterday when she read of his death
she had been unable to recall his face,

as if it was someone else she hardly knew,
who had loved him all summer till war came

and he made her go, with the suitcase, the shawl
and the roses he threw as the last boat pulled away

But now, fingering the silk, she remembered –
his touch, his voice, the unforgiving light,

that twist of pine and incense on the air,
the nagging bells, and how, as they swam out

beyond the rocks, the sea grew turquoise,
silvered with small fish, and deepened into blue.

THE GLASS DOOR

We get round to it it at last
though at night
for reasons which aren't clear,
no music, no flowers,
both of us squashed in here
behind this small table
in front of a bunch of strangers
and I'm wearing stilettos
and the hat with the black feathers
that always makes you laugh
but, when I close in for the kiss
you've gone
and it takes forever,
running through a chain
of shuttered rooms
before I find you again
on the far side
of this locked glass door
and I've lost the hat
and you're standing there
on some kind of terrace
with a women in a red dress,
both with your backs to me,
and when I tap on the pane,
the two of you turn
to stare back, unsmiling,
and I call out your name
and break through the glass
but you're not there any more,
just a lot of blood
on my hands and everywhere,
everywhere.

CHANCE MEETING

How good it was to see you last night,
so unexpectedly and after so long
but you seemed thinner than usual
inside your uniform and more concerned
with official business than I remember.

Did you notice that I too have changed,
how I waited, making no sign, no demands,
until at last you came across the room
to ask, with that familiar urgency,
if I would return after midnight?

Too late, things are different now.
I can forgive you for dying before me
but you no longer have the right
to keep me hanging around like this
and to waste so much of my time.

MIDNIGHT IN THE EMBASSY

The Minister of Defence
is up and dancing, chasséeing
across the parquet floor
on feet smaller than mine,
his hands, fluid, jointless,
beckoning me to him,
spinning me into the dance
as he explains that the music
tells a very old story
of a man who is torn
between his long-time wife
and a ripe young girl.

The Ambassador nods
and plies his bow,
the princess taps in time,
drawing in her crimson skirt
while the one-legged piper
and the grinning boy on the drum
play faster, faster
to a flutter of applause
and half-supressed laughter
from the rows of women
on stiff gilt chairs.

But now a girl I do not know
leaps from her seat,
tossing back her lemon hair,
and the Minister of Defence
turns this way and that
between us, rolling his eyes,
extending a hand
first to one, then the other
as the watching women

grow ecstatic, and you, love,
impassive in the front row,
look straight ahead – for this is,
after all, a very old story.

MR IRRESISTIBLE

So it's come to this,
I hang about all day, wasting
my time, wait for you,
whisper your name, shiver
at the thought of your caresses
until at last you swagger in,
late and shameless, making
one of your brief appearances
and staking out your claim.

Worse, I confess this too –
I sleep badly now, dreaming
of you throughout the night,
you and those ambiguous,
half-cold embraces of yours
which make me sweat and tremble.

I trace your finger's touches
on my skin, so light, so gentle,
yet see how they've left me
webbed over with fine lines.

I lick the sticky, barely-
perceptible smears
with which you streak
and mark me as your own,
I taste the stains
that cling like faded bruises.

How arrogant you are,
how well, how quickly
you have come to know me,
yet sometimes, even now
at this last hour, I hesitate,
drawing back, afraid.

But what do you care?
Indifferent, sure of yourself,
you wander off and disappear
for a while, aware that few
can deny you for long.

Ultimately, you will not take no
for an answer, persistent,
irresistible Death, my last
and only faithful lover.
I swear I'll burn for you yet.

MAKING FOR THE LOWER FIELD

> *'There is strong evidence for the idea that memories are created afresh each time we experience them'* (from a report on the application of Chaos Theory to human memory)

Hey oop! Hey oop!
We are making for the lower field,
the sun nothing more
than a gold rim round the distant elms.
I swing on the blue gate's hinge-end
as it whines open
and the shorthorns bucket through
in a reek of mud and hot shit,
oblivious to the future
which is staggering,
just so many holes in the head.

Hey oop! Hey oop!
I bang the pail, they come on by
amiably enough,
these long-dead stirks and heifers,
barging over the plashed ground,
hips jaunty and gilded with pollen.
They swing pert heads
and roll their thick-lashed eyes,
still flirty under those veils
of may and elder – but look, now
they kick up their heels and rocket off,
high-tailing it into the sunset.

TIME MACHINE

Click-click, click-clack,
Harold Threlkeld, the farmer's son,
comes swinging milk-cans
across the fields, over the stile,
down the cinder path to the kitchen.

Click-click, click-clack,
clogs in the cobbled yard,
the Atco stutters across the lawn,
hot water pipes are creaking
as they do first thing in the mornings,
there is a dog barking
and the rising stutter of a straying hen
in the woods behind the house
where her eggs will slowly rot away
among the mosses, wood-sorrel,
and purple-veined windflowers.

Upright in a spindle-backed chair
he is into his third cup of tea
and halfway through
the *Manchester Guardian*,
while she, humming under her breath,
busy on my First-Communion frock,
is heel-and-toeing it at the treadle
of her mother's gold-scrolled Singer
on which, *click-click, click-clack*,
my daughter sews her wedding dress.

R I WITH SISTER BRIDGET, 1943

We'd got to the bit about four sins
which cry to Heaven for vengeance
so I put up my hand
to ask what one of them was, exactly,
the Sin of Sodom,
because I'd never heard of it
and really wanted to know
but the minute the words were out
it was clear I'd hit a no-no
for there was Sister Bridget
with eyes like gob-stoppers,
face red as a fire bucket
and for once not a word out of her
until somebody laughed
when she sucked in her cheeks,
rolled her eyes up to Heaven
as if to seek divine aid
and hissed that it was something
so wicked, so terrible,
that nobody knew what it was
which blew our minds,
I mean scary, and after that
she had no more trouble with any of us
but it left me anxious –
next time I went to Confession,
I hedged my bets and confessed to it,
whatever it was –
better be safe than sorry.

IN THE POTTING SHED

He stoops over the slatted shelves,
absorbed, content, lips pursed
to produce his speciality,
a sort of hissing whistle
through his teeth
which maddens her,
a long, long trail a-winding
or bits and pieces
from *The Merry Widow* –
Vilia and that waltz

an awkward sort of man who,
thinking himself alone here
amongst the clay pots
and sacks of compost,
becomes tender, hesitant,
fingers hovering delicately
over the wooden seed-trays

but already we have sensed
from the look of things,
from her drooping lips,
the wistful piano
late at night and the way
she undresses, stiffly,
beneath a dressing gown,
that delicacy does not
come into it much
between them,

that it could only have been
some unimaginable,
never to be mentioned,
cack-handed fumblings
in the musty dark
that seeded eight of us

BULL'S EYES

Once it grabbed him when halfway
up the stairs. It was the roar,
that billowing roar, that huddled us
behind the bannisters, furiously
sucking bull's-eyes, eight silent watchers,
at a cage marked dangerous.
Lumbago, someone whispered.

Our mother fetched buckets, sponges
and a clutch of red hot-water bottles,
having a great belief in warmth
although by now they slept apart,
stiff-limbed in separate rooms.

It was an hour before the spasm passed
and she could free him. I have forgotten
the rest of the day, remembering
only that roar, the dripping sweat
and the look in his eyes, knowing
that he was stuck there, as usual,
just halfway to something he wanted.

MY FATHER DYING

He took his time over it, dying slowly
in fireside chairs, blind, spilling whisky
and the detritus of nine decades
over the worn carpets of dust-balled rooms
where pendulums edged him towards night
but if you asked him how he was, he'd sigh
it's time the angels came for me.

Yet waiting, he remembered
and his foot would tap to silent waltzes
as he saw again the gas-lit drives, the girls
he'd played at tennis, the smiling boys
in school photographs, their sepia ranks
now whitening on the Somme.

With his guns laid by, cold
and oiled in leather cases, his fingers
coiled round drooping cigarettes
as the past rolled by in patches
like hill mist on the black moors
he'd loved since he was a boy.

There were bonfires for the Jubilee
(belee, belee – belee, belee, belee)
and Ladysmith, Old Nursey wept
when Queen Victoria died, Pavlova
danced and Gigli sang.

Each time he talked, the patterns changed,
the kaleidoscope shifted until, in bed at last,
he'd lie in foetal innocence, brushed,
washed, pyjammaed, his penis curled,
a soft toy in his hand. It seemed a small,
a gentle thing to father eight of us.

GOING HOME

Inching north, as if glued to the track,
the train's caught up in all the cloying green,
bogged down in birdsong and the thick dun earth,
the slack rhythms of the afternoon
and the bland softness of the southern light,
let me, this one last time, be not late back,

stuck in this time-warp, travelling again
on holiday from school, crossing off names,
Bletchley, Stafford, Crewe, like so many dates
on a classroom calendar, clawing up
the country's long and undulating spine
to these lean hills until, at last, the train

pulls into Preston. No ghostly porters come
no smiling Tom or Lol to take my bags
and say that I have grown. The rain still falls
as chill, fingering at my shirt
and flattening my hair – I had forgotten
how our northern gutters sing with water.

For years you've said it's time the angels came
for you and oh, how I wish you angels now,
the comfort their enfolding wings
might bring, you sad, beloved, difficult
old man, my blind and angry father,
dying alone and thinking me to blame

for it, for these last, bewildered days
spent here amongst strangers, the unfamiliar
voices, the alien hands assaulting you
with needles, pills and plastic tubes, as heart
and kidneys pack it in, until you leave
with just one bitter valedictory phrase.

MARBLE

It's a sad pilgrimage, walking here again
on my old escape route from the stale
and foetid air of your last room. Today
the park's a shadow-world of half-tones –
greys, soft browns, a hint of aubergine. Mist
blurs the margins of the park and turns
the osiers on the farther shore to ghosts.
Here in the sunken garden I sit alone
with pale Affection and with drooping Grief,
whose chaste white bodies have been sprayed
with crude dabs of black hair. I mourn
the violation, how the paint has stained
these small, dank triangles between their thighs.
It's a year now since the hurricane which felled
a dozen trees around your house and so began
the slow countdown to your end. We watched
your life shrink within its narrow margins, as days
smudged into weeks and weeks blurred into months,
October through to Christmas, on to May, watched
you bow your head between your swollen knees,
one angry, stick-like arm beating upon the bed.
I want to die, you said, time and again,
and we believed you, could only hold you,
stroke your thin hair, your fragile skin, feeling
that insubstantial tegument stretched tight
against the bone as, helpless, we saw you sink
into a shadow-world of low-watt bulbs,
drawn curtains, screens. Being blind
you took the daily violation of our hands
as we washed and turned you, dried your cold limbs –
just like marble, we said and saw, at that,
you raise a still-graceful finger to your chin
in an unconscious act of coquetry,
the last gesture of an Edwardian belle.

NIGHT WATCH

The warmth within this room has closed your eyes.
You sink back in your pillows, folding in
like a spent flower. Tender as a gardener, I see
how even in sleep, your clawed and knotted fingers
creep like old, bared roots across the crumpled linen
of the bed towards your rosary. I keep the night with you
remembering – how you watched over me so many nights,
were always there, and how it felt even before I knew
words that could hold, define the memory,
when your hand held mine, thrust
between bars of the cot beside your bed;
when the dustfish swam in the rock-pool of our room,
through the brown fronds of your hair. When I
was like a bud, enfurled, well-swaddled against the cold,
with scarves and coat, leggings, boots; a buttonhook world
made safe for your eighth, your last, your 'Tantony.
Behind hands, neighbours whispered 'She'll never rear her'
but slim and white as new-peeled sallies, your fingers
seeded grapes, sieved fruit, brewed and stewed soup,
beef-tea, set junkets, jellies for me, persuaded me to live.

Now I lay out this tray for you with flowers and silver,
linen, lace, cut toast in crustless strips, hold
soup and sherry to your lips, persuading you to stay.
At night, I stop three or four times outside your door,
hands cupped like shells to shield the light
and hold your ebbing breath against my ear. Your death
hovers between us, waiting to be recognised
but I won't look, wrap you up against the cold
of your old adversary, button him out and hook you
to me, still need to hold your hand – *Timor mortis
conturbat me.* Today the weather changed, frost threatens,
frets the wind. I linger in the garden, check ties
and stakes, mulch or wrap sacking round the vulnerable

then, as the light goes, come inside to stack the fire
and draw your curtains early. When you slip, briefly,
into sleep, I wander through the house from room to room,
looking for something or other I have lost, can't settle.
You used to call me Fidgety Phil, do you remember,
and how I could never say goodnight?

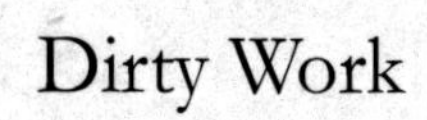

Dirty Work

TRIZONIA

O most excellent donkey who,
not having heard of the sleep button,
woke me three times this morning
with your ancient and execrable lament,
do you bemoan the start
of your overburdened day
and the end of your brief night's rest
in this unpromising patch of scrub
or do you, perhaps, grieve for me
who today must leave this incomparable islet
where there are neither cars
nor motorcycles, where nothing
very much happens, apart
from the occasional birth or marriage
and the rather more frequent deaths,
where there is little to see, just Iannis
repainting the peeling mermaid
on his taverna, and his grandmother
taking a broom to the six hollow-ribbed cats
who have stolen yet another chicken-leg,
and the three old men who,
having finished their backgammon
and the last of the ouzo, now take
the sun's path home across the harbour
in a boat as blue as that clump of scabious
you are considering?

I WANT TO TELL HER

I want to tell her,
the woman opposite me,
look, loosen up a little,
don't let on, don't
let them see, nobody
loves a loser – because
it's too old for her,
that drawn and weary face,
that turned-down mouth,
those seen-it-all eyes –
but now she leans forward
and I see her breasts
and they are beautiful –
and I want to tell her, look,
men will always love you
for your beautiful breasts
and, with a bit of luck,
one of them, one day,
will take your face
between his hands, and
with a bit of luck, will kiss
your down-turned mouth
back into laughter.

JULIA'S DOVES

i.m. Julia Casterton

we reach the long-planned
rendezvous and find you gone

we search for your doves
but they are nowhere to be seen

there is only the grief of gulls
the scent of pine, the hot sun

and white-fingered waves
clawing at the rocks below

instead of a wreath
we pick these flowers

the small wild flowers
of Finisterre

yellow bell-flowers, gentians
wild thyme, white campion

and cast them out to sea, watch
as the wind lifts and scatters them

towards the Atlantic horizon
like birds, like butterflies, like words

FINAL REDUCTIONS IN THE SOFA WORKSHOP

He changes things slowly, one by one,
a feeling of disloyalty each time –

a new kettle when the old one blows,
a blue enamel egg-pan to replace

the one she burned dry, time and again,
a single bed, room now for a desk

where he can lay out his stamps –
she would never have allowed that –

his niece buys him a gramophone,
he plays his 78s: Gershwin, Berlin,

Rodgers and Hammerstein, Cole
Porter, smoke gets in his eyes,

she was the cream in his coffee,
she was the salt in his stew.

You could do with a new sofa,
his niece says, frowning at the stain,

and a chair while you're about it,
there's a sale on till Saturday.

Sofa, so good says the sign –
but he doesn't get the joke,

carefully, he sits in every one,
makes sure he can get up again,

two hours later he has settled
on cherry-red linen, pleased

with the brightness – his niece
doubts it is really suitable –

This is our Miranda range, Sir,
the salesgirl says, *a very good choice* –

she smiles at him, leans
forward to present the bill –

and free delivery – her blouse gapes,
breasts overflow the bra's half-shells,

he stares, cannot help himself,
he longs, longs to touch them,

the niece tugs him to his feet,
buttons him into his coat.

BEECH HILL

for I.M. Birtwistle, 1918 – 2006

Last night the loon flew over from Long Pond
to Echo Lake – and onwards, far beyond

our darkening woods, mourning as she went –
now, after these six long hot hours, hard spent

in hacking out a path down to the shore
I take the Beech Hill road, past Charlie's door

then on by Sunset Farm towards Beech Cliff
to hear her call again, but nearer still, as if

to join, in counterpoint, the coyote's wild grief
with mine – that you're not here. I watch the brief

trajectories of passing satellites
between the falling stars, see, as the lights

of Todd's old pick-up brush across the lawn,
the soft and startled eyes of doe and fawn.

DAVY GRAHAM AT NICK'S DINER, 1964

Here's my baby, dressed in white,
if your love's for me, won't you stay the night?

One a.m. in Ifield Road,
Chelsea's paving-stones
are hanging on to the heat,
the Diner's hopping,
a solipsistic bubble
on the point of implosion,
but Serafina's there,
and she's cooling it.

Why's my baby dressed in black?
well now baby, won't you please come back?

Tonight he starts with Gary Davis –
in the kitchen the mayonnaise
curdles, Italian Joe sweats,
making his nightly grab for Sasha
as she collects two Steaks Tartare
and four Oeufes Florentine
for Table Six – as usual,
she knees him.

Oh baby, baby, please come quick,
this old Cocaine's making me sick –

The new waiter, an Adam Faith
look-alike, tips a bottle of wine
over Reggie Kray and a merchant
banker – there's a hush, Nick hovers,
charms, smoothes things –
Davy leans over the guitar,
long legs akimbo, candlelight
lurking in his hair.

Here's my baby, dressed in blue,
well now, lover, what's the matter with you?

At the till, Sasha sulks,
for now, having given them
a sweet How Long Blues,
wandered his way
through Muddy Waters, Bach,
Art Blakey and Big Bill Broonzy,
he is finishing off with *Anji* –
which she hates.

Tomorrow he'll move on,
to Bunji's or the Troubadour,
play them folk, blues – and maybe
something else, something
that is far, far beyond.

SINGLES NIGHT AT THE MADRUGADA

All right, all right, if you insist – third turn on the left into Deadpan
Alley, any time after midnight, knock twice, whistle the first three
bars of, say, the second track on The Return of Dr. Octagon, and
Rat-Butt Billy will let you in if he likes the tune and the look of you –
don't try too hard, he's got a nose for the prick, the prat, the poseur
and the ponce – just take things easy, a nod's OK, but for God's
sake don't smile – Billy has this thing about guys who smile – his
wife dumped him for the drummer from Hot Black Stardust, the
thin one, with the sea-snake tattoos, who's had his teeth fixed – and
watch out for the strobes, they may reveal more than you'd care for,
hard to describe – let's put it this way, I've seen sights in there that
are best forgotten, so don't say I didn't warn you – one more thing –
you can trust Chitty Moll, Bang-Bang and the Siamese twins but if a
baby-faced tranny turns up in a silver shift and high-heeled sneakers,
and offers you a white rose, get out of there fast, I mean fast and
don't look back – believe me.

DIRTY WORK

They have been here before us,
those other ones,
leaving a resonance in the air,
a bloom of fingermarks
on the furniture,
burns on the fumed oak.

Did they too put their cases down
side by side on the thin carpet,
lock the door, blow dust and hair
from the bedside table,
think the stain on the ceiling
looked like Australia?

You unwrap champagne,
I open caviar, we share one spoon,
it takes more than a hard bed
and a dim lamp to deter us
but the bottle looks awkward here,
like gentry at a village wedding.

When the last bubbles burst
we stand hand in hand
at the window. Look, you say
even the glass is dirty
and you breathe on it,
tracing the usual patterns,
twined initials, arrows, hearts.

PORTRAIT OF MISS FREDA MARWOOD

(taken in the Amy Sharples Studio, Blackburn, 1919)

To her father's exasperation
she wears the sort of clothes

favoured by Miss Sackville-West –
a type of woman he has no time for –

beneath a wide-brimmed felt hat,
she turns towards me an enigmatic

half-profile above her softly-tailored shirt,
loose tie, goose-winged breeches,

buttoned gaiters, those neat
well-polished boots – a woman

caught by the throat, choking
in the closeness of gas-lit rooms,

endless croquet summers
and charades of winter, stuck there

with a blithely selfish father, three
shell-shocked brothers and an ailing

sister, stuck here in this family album,
time-warped in that long denial.

UNLACING MY MOTHER

You don't need a corset, we protest,
exhausted, struggling at midnight

to untie the knots she's made
with her blind, swollen-jointed

fingers in the tangled strings –
as always, she replies, *but darlings,*

it's so comforting – she sighs,
and clasps her hands defensively

across her breasts, while behind her,
we roll eyes together. It seems

to take an age before she's freed,
swapping whalebone and pink satin

for a flower-sprigged nightdress.
We smooth sheets, rearrange pillows,

settle her in and then lean forward to
receive her kisses, her *God bless*

and those same thumb-traced crosses
made upon our foreheads every night

when we were children. Now we, in turn,
dim the lights and leave her door ajar.

THRELKELD'S BULL

At the beginning it is the tulip curtains, the light pouring through them, the dustfish rising and falling in the light, and the halo of the mother's hair as she leans over the child's cot

or perhaps the beginning is in the pram under the apple-trees, the shifting of green and gold overhead, the brief warmth of the wet flannel-sheet beneath the child, the whistling of Harold, the milk-boy, as he climbs over the stile

and either way, next it is *Holy Holy Holy*, with the father holding the child to his shoulder, *Lord God Almighty*, sings the father, beating the child's back softly, heels rocking on the nursery floor, flames flicker-flack behind the brass-trimmed fireguard

then Hilda and Mollie are singing in the kitchen, *Moonatsy, shining so bright, guide my lover tonight, Moonatsy*, they sing, for they are walking-out with Peadar and Danny, over for the haymaking, and the child watches as each man drinks a half-gallon of cold tea, straight from the can, their cheeks cherry-bright but Martha Thorpe says that is TB roses

later still, in the lower meadow, red-white-and-blue bunting flitters between the elm trees, *God Save Our Noble King* sing the schoolchildren, and bob-haired, black-stockinged girls skip over the twisting ropes, *one-pertater, two-pertater, three-pertater four* –

and Amos Fazackerley wins the Sack, Enoch Fazackerkey wins the Egg-and-Spoon, together they win the Three-legged, which isn't fair, and the child cries when her sister drops her near the end of the Wheelbarrow-race, sure she should have won –

Mr Povey-the-vicar says a prayer for the Prince of Wales, Lady-Mardy-from-the-Hall gives out prizes, poor old Batty-Patty, whose love died in the trenches, runs here, there and everywhere, while Miss Gornall-from-the-school pours out fresh lemonade into green crackle-glass tumblers and rations the children to one each –

soon after that it is bedtime, a tin-bath by the fire, warm towels, hot milk, iced biscuits, and *eeh, that Mrs. Simpson*, says Martha, knotting cotton rags into the child's hair – *who's Mrs. Simpson*, the child asks, asleep before the answer

and she wakes to the sound of clogs in the cobbled yard and the Atco on the lawn leaving dark stripes in the dew, and this is the day, the day after the Jubilee fete, that Harold's dad goes into the pen and is gored by Threlkeld's black bull

so the next week candles are lit in St. Joseph's, the red lamp shines over the tabernacle, *Introibo ad altare Dei, I will go unto the altar of God*, says Father Livsey, *Ad Deum qui laetificat juventutem meum, to God who gives joy to my youth*, say the altar-boys, but the choir sings *De profundis*, and where now is the joy? Where is it?

SARDINES

Her first house-party
and long frock, but now
she is stuck here in the dark,
crammed into a linen cupboard
with a man she doesn't know
who's at least forty
and he's wearing tails, plus
some sort of cummerbund
and she is praying –

Please, please, Holy Mother Mary,
let me be found by the others,
by someone, anyone else
before he does it again,
before he sticks his tongue
so far into my mouth
that I'm going to be sick. –

God, but you're sweet, he says,
pushing his thighs against hers,
you smell like chrysanthemums –
but with her nose jammed
into his stiff shirtfront,
all she can smell is the starch,
his tar breath, her wet taffeta,
and the stinking fish-sweat.

THANKS TO YOU, CHARLIE CHESTER

Sheep's eyes, sand pies, a watch without
a spring, you can buy a pomegranate too
in the old bazaar in Cairo –

Broke as usual, we ate out
somewhere in the back streets
of Al Qahirah, the triumphant city,
bravely trying labna, koshary, leleq,
basbusa, pestered by swarms
of doe-eyed boys, clamouring
to sell us yet more food, coins, scarabs,
their sisters, the pyramids – until
we escaped them and, dodging
between the swaying waiters
with coffee trays aloft, we slipped
at last into the gloom of Shepheard's
and its weary grandeur, into
the cold welcome of its marble floors,
with no good reason that I could see
for the choice, except, perhaps,
that once, during the war,
you had jumped from its balcony –
a boasted act that, if true,
I secretly thought silly.

Mamadan, Ramadan, everything in style,
genuine, bedouin, carpets with a pile,
in the old bazaar in Cairo –

The perfect place for a first fuck,
you said, positioning me on the bed,
but to be honest with you, and no,
I didn't tell you this at the time –
being a virgin, I had no expectations –
with hindsight, neither the place
nor the act itself were all that

perfect: the bed uncomfortable
and the sex being over
almost before it began, so what
I remember most about the week –
apart from those earrings we bought
in the City of the Dead's suq al guma'a,
plus the flies, feluccas, falafel
and Fahid – is that stupid song
you sang, prancing starkers
round our room, my knickers
on your head, doing what you
swore was a sand dance, a one-man
Wilson, Keppel and Betty.

THE SWEET SCENT OF HAWTHORN

you say the moon too is horned
but, as I see it from this angle, she is a raised eyebrow
and perhaps we have surprised her

for the cows too seem mildly astonished,
wide-eyed at our intricacies, chewing things over,
puzzled by such ineptitude

they circle nearer, their broad flanks
hung with castanets of dung that click, click, click
to our quickening rhythm

there is a lot of head-tossing and heavy breathing
something sweet and foxy in the air
our sweat mashing with the scent of hawthorn

HARVEST MOON

When he left her in January
she was as empty as the new moon.

In February, her veined breasts
grew tender, the nipples hardened,

and stood out from their dark areolas
while the days lengthened and greened up.

By the end of April her white belly fluttered,
became streaked with blue, curving

smooth and fertile as a mushroom. Through
June, July and August she dreamed time away,

drifting about the silent house like tumbleweed,
rootless, limbs heavy, her hands

pressed to the aching hollow of her back
but on the first night in September she rose

and sailed out proudly, round and swollen
as a harvest moon, to greet her daughter.

LA MATANZA

Madrid 2004

Look how the unshrouded dead
are flung between the wreckage layers
of destroyed compartments
their somehow-unbloodied faces
strung along wires and twisted
steel. That woman there, Dante
and Hieronymus would know her
at once, head askew, the eyes'
indignant upward stare
the surprised O of her mouth
while this one here, it seems
she lies asleep, *una bella*
durmiente, behind these metal
thorns – but think how they woke
today like us, dragging themselves
from dreams or lovers' arms
took showers, put coffee on
chose shoes and shirts and jeans
or frocks to wear, turned back
to wave at those who stayed behind
or laughed and blew them kisses
then ran to catch their trains.

LETTER FROM RATHCOURSEY

Sweetheart, I write to tell you how the sun
has glazed the distant stubble fields with light
and that the old zinc bucket which you filled
with weeds still squats upon the grey stone steps
before the painted door. What would you call
that colour? Dusty, or slate, or maybe
breast-of-dove? Rathcoursey blue will have
to serve for now. Then also, you should know,
ten Tortoiseshells, a Cabbage White and two
Red Admirals have spread their wings upon
the purple buddleia which grows beside
our wind-raked washing line and, yes, the wren
still flits among the fennel's rattling seeds
but more than this, the house and I, the ducks,
geese, sun, butterflies and wren –
even the dented bucket – all long for your
return. Ridiculous, you'll say, but no less true
for that. Time creeps, the bread is proved,
come back, come back, we wait for you,
the Aga kettle sings, the whiskey's poured.

ON MY BIRTHDAY I TRAVEL IN EXPECTATION

Meet me under the warthog, you said –
but my plane is late, it spirals down
towards Kennedy as the turquoise eyes
of countless swimming pools
stare up at me, the two guys
at Immigration have cold-sores,
and the yellow cab takes it slow
on the ride in. Fourth of July,
not yet dark, but already thousands
cluster along the East River
while kids who look too young to drive
lean out of beat-up Chevys,
waving beer cans, anticipating
the premature eruption of rockets.
By the time we reach West 44th
I know more about the driver's wife
than I care to, a poster admonishes
Honey, if he don't wear a condom,
he ain't getting' any. It's three hours
since my e.t.a, the light has vanished,
a porter unlocks the door, lets me in
to a pillared hall, calls your room.
Everything is closed, even the Late-Nite
Sushi is barred to us; side by side
we wait for the elevator in silence,
the stuffed head of the warthog
shot by a Roosevelt hangs on the wall
above us, the look on his face
somehow familiar. A window lights up
in the offices across the street,
there's a cough from the next room,
the air-conditioning has failed –
tired, thirsty, hungry, we make do
with peanuts and cola from the mini-bar –
it becomes clear that sex is off –
now I long for Smirnoff, root beer,

chowder, oyster-crackers, dough-balls,
buffalo-wings, biscuits-and-gravy,
meat-loaf, scrapple, stuffed quahogs,
apple pie, brownies, a Hershey bar,
a BLT – tomorrow I'll call Maja, together
we'll sit on those steps outside the Met,
buy hot dogs, lick the mustard.

PAY DAY

The last day of May – overnight
the garden has opened out,

firethorns drip cream
along the boundary fence,

poppies rise up
from glaucous leaves,

spread split red skirts,
reveal their black centres,

their secret places, silk filaments,
the puckered green of their sex,

everywhere such generosity –
and you, love, closed tight, tight

as a miser's tight fist on pay day,
you, too, now open yourself to me.

DINNER IN LA CORUÑA

Old hands at this, we order *percebes, minchas,*
cigales, cabrachos and *lamprejas* – but this
does not please our waiter who insists
we use the English version of the menu
from which he warmly recommends
Scrambles of Tender Garlics, Wide Open
Olives, A Sort of Fish, Weak Rice
with Snips of Lobster, Toast of Turnip Greens
with Hat of St. Simon and Comb of Pork,
A Small Bowl of Rice with Tasty, Tasty Bacon,
and – with a final flourish, he conjures up for us
Today's Specials – Galician Back-of-the-Knee
or Warm Escalabola with Cod's Tears –
in a last bid for independence, we settle
for A Crispy of King Prawns, followed by
Pale Ice-Cream with Saucy Oranges and Scum.

POT LUCK

If she hadn't met
Lavinia in Ken High
and if Lavinia hadn't asked her
to share a flat in Chelsea
with Claire and Thomasina
and if Claire's brother Roger
just out of Sandhurst
hadn't brought his best friend
Rupert Pratt-Mather
back for supper one night
she might never have lived
unhappily ever after.

TAPAS

Despite everything you're such an optimist
while I, on the other hand,
expect the worst and usually find it.

Tonight, for instance, the calamares
that you ordered are quite perfect
while my patatas bravas have lost heart

but I eat them, noting that the last two years
have turned your hair to grey
and how, surprisingly, it suits you

and how too, in the murky candlelight
of this overpriced wine-bar,
your eyes are quick and blue as garfish

and it's kind of you to ask, but there have been,
after all, more than twenty-two years
of occasional meetings and overseas calls,

of wry amusement at each other's amourettes –
it is surely too late to start, and so,
though you kiss me on the lips and eyelids

in that familiar and intimate way of an old lover,
though we stand here like gobsmacked teenagers,
muchas gracias, but no.

LEGACES

And for you, my rosewood sewing-box,
she said – now it stands, polished and delicate

beside my bed, a neat sarcophagus
in this untidy room, so out of place here

that for weeks I hesitate to open it,
disturb what she last put away

but today I pluck up courage, blowing
off the dust as one who brushes softly

through layers of sand to find small
artefacts in the detritus of a tomb.

What power the everyday possessions
of the dead have to move us –

I finger an ivory spool, a needle-case,
her scissors, silver thimbles,

these twists of silk and cotton thread,
hear her singing Gershwin,

catch the soft, sad, violet scent
of Pivet's Floramie.

ON DUXON HILL

Look, Tiggs, a plover's nest –
the thumb-stick points,

dripping with mud,
marsh-marigolds and weed.

Another step would crush
these khaki eggs, four of them

lying freckled and exposed
in this fragile saucer

of dry grass. My hand held tight
in his, I'm safe, wrapped up

in the warm smell of tweed
and Gold Flake, beneath

the peewits' ever-circling wings.
He is at ease here on the hill,

well-camouflaged, a speckled shape
in brown plus-fours, his anger

drained away, a grizzled ram,
moving surely now

through the beloved landscape,
an old tup with his lamb.

A QUESTION OF GREEN PARAKEETS

There they go, the green parakeets –
that sudden flash against the blue,
that vapour trail of squawks –
Como las mujeres chafarderas,
Antonio says, and his wife, Maria,
laughs, lashing out at him
with the wooden olive-spoon –
he ducks, of course – but enough
of this, what concerns me is
the reality of now, or should I say
the unreality, you decide – and if
time is circular as you maintain,
have the parakeets just arrived
in this particular plaça, at noon
precisely, or just left, merely
to return next year, next century,
next millennium or when?
And not only the parakeets,
but you and I, Antonio, our table,
Maria, the raised olive-spoon –
OK, think of it another way,
remember how, in London,
all those years ago, we'd party
on the Circle Line, filling our glasses
in that pub there used to be –
what was its name – on the platform
at Sloane Square, everyone air-kissing,
drinking gin and orangeade
or Moroccan wine, while the train
carried us round, and back to where
we'd started from, how we'd refill
our flasks before careering on – it
worries me – are we still circling there,
the then held with the now
and today's parakeets in some
space-time continuum? God only knows,

I'm no philosopher, no physicist,
forget I asked – those bloody birds,
they're back again – look, another
glass of txacoli, my friend, or try
one of these, Maria's poverones,
she swears they're freshly made.

A Scent of Winter

GREEN WINE

He tempts her with Portugal in spring.
I can't, she says, not having stayed before
in a hotel with anyone but her husband.
He laughs, kisses her, pointing out that
there are four hundred bedrooms, so who
will know or care? This being a question
to which she has no answer, they go,
oblivious to the Carnation Revolution,
bewildered to find their hotel empty,
terraces deserted, salt pool unruffled,
to dine alone in a chandeliered ballroom
where a trio of forlorn women play
selections from long dead musicals. *This
soup's good*, he says; she stabs her plate,
an ill-conceived stew of pork, beans and
shellfish. *It can't get any worse*, she thinks
but all week the sun's too hot, the beach
too far; they trail from one sad bar or café
to the next, weary of fado, the endless
bacalhau, those sickly egg yolk docinhos
whipped up, she imagines, by sour-faced
nuns. *We should never go back*, he says
on the last night. *I should never have come*
she thinks, sticky with guilt and sugar
which she tries to rinse away in vinho
verde. And later, it will not be this meal,
his sleeping face and priapic body or
his unfaithful mouth she remembers
but how, slipping in through shutters,
the sunlight stained everything.

HOW IT IS

i.m. Sam Alexander MC

Trestles slid away, folded
and put aside, candles snuffed
the singing stops, the music
dies, mourners drift off
and regroup by the gate.

Dear God, there seems
so little now to show for it all
nothing but a rolled-up flag
a scatter of wreaths, a bugle call
this shock of fresh-dug earth.

FOXHOLES

Back from France by small boats
and night trains
the last one stopping
to let him down in the wet fields
where he'd pick his way
through the warm breath of cows,
tensing at every vixen's bark,
owl call, twig-snap and leaf rustle,
at something half seen
behind the bramble mound,
then over the stone stile
like a final obstacle in an old game,
up the potholed drive,
past the duck pond
and in at last to the kitchen
where some mornings
we'd find him there asleep,
spark out on the dog-haired sofa.

In the creased photograph
beside his mother's bed
he leans against her,
nineteen, thin inside his uniform,
the bloodstained bandage
tight against his hair
and for years after there were times
when the dreams came back
till we grew used to it, waking
to the shouts and screams,
to the glimpses of him
struggling naked
in his damp and foxy bed

CONVALLARIA

i.m. L M K, b & d 13.5.57

Watching this barren scratch
of earth, I could swear they've
gone, yet all at once they're
back, those green rabbit-ears
thrusting up, spreading
faster, thicker than one could
imagine. It was May when
I lost you, after that raw night
when an indifferent world
turned over in its sleep
and I never once held you
but the next day everyone
brought lilies of the valley
until the air was thick and sickly
with their scent. For long after,
I'd not allow them near me
but now, all these years on,
I've come to terms. Look love,
I've planted them here for you
beneath this red camellia, see how
they thrive there in the shade.

ALLOW ME TO INTRODUCE MYSELF

Professor Alegna Amaranthus,
Doctor of Psychic Medicine,
Specialist in Spiritual Healing,
Tarot, Scrying and I-Ching.
Are you unhappy in life, love,
work, relationships? Do bad
dreams, negative thoughts,
malign forces, Kala Judoo,
Voodoo, the Evil Eye or any
of the Black Arts trouble you?
Seventh child of a Seventh child,
long experienced in the occult,
omens, dreams, auguries, dowsing,
hypnotism, divination, exorcism,
psychometry, aereomancy,
cleromancy, necromancy, skilled
in sortilege and haruscipation:
tea-leaves, entrails, movements
of birds, droppings of feral goats,
peregrinations of spider-crabs;
in the laying-on of hands, spells,
decoction and application
of herbs. For 15 euros I heal hearts,
improve fertility, calm minds,
cure gout and baldness, remove
unwanted fat, varicose veins,
surplus hair, moles, birthmarks,
verrucas, warts; no problem
too big or too small. Visit
my House of Spirits, let me read
your palm, tell your fortune –
call today for a better tomorrow.

SALBITXADA

night closes in, husky
with sex and charcoal
circling the grill's raw eye

grind of techno
from La Macarena, flasks
of orujo, patxaran

the calçots, flaccid
blackened, lie on a tegula
the red sauce grainy

pebrots de nyores, ail
tomàquets, ametiles
y avellanes, sal, pebre

we peel off charred leaves
from pallid phalluses
dunk, suck them clean.

LARK RISE AT BRANCASTER

Sea turf, cinquefoil, thrift; below us
a criss-crossed sea's serrated edge
frets at the sand-cliff's foot. Spread
eagled in the sun's warm crook
we lie thyme pillowed. Then close
a sudden ecstasy: a rise, a soar
a flight of joy, euphoric babbling
of song, its soloist far beyond our
sight, and more join in, the sky
becomes one vast delirious arch
of fluid praise, a blue celestial peon
so that we too become borne up
in ravishment, ferocious bliss, this
thermal exaltation of the larks.

WIND THE DECEIVER

blows sweet then sour,
warm then chill, whines
down the world's rat-runs,
wuthers in the high chimneys
of deserted mill-towns,
whistles through ossicles –
incus, malleus, stapes –
its cold breath sucking air
from the lungs. Wind presses
icy lips to the vagrant, is dry
as a dying man's mouth,
wet as Cullam Marshes.

Wind says *Call me Helm, Foehn,*
Mistral, Briza. Call me Kaver,
Tramontana, Coromell. Call me
Diablo, Contrastes. I know
and fear it, how it brings
Sahara sand and volcanic ash
to London's streets, ice
to the rigging of fishing boats,
whips snow into whiteouts
flattens harvests, wrestles
slates from the rooftops,
Quercus from the earth.

PARSON'S PLEASURE

Looking back through the near-perfect
crescent of that first sweet post-war
slice of picnic cantaloup we ride again
the potholed back-way there, free-wheeling
our Raleighs, battered sit-up-and-begs
skidding and falling down the steep hill
to where the Isis idles green by Magdalen Bridge
and lingers for a while in Parson's Pleasure.
Do withered Dons with balding heads
and shriveled thighs still peer through
knotholes into Dames' Delight, watching
as we shriek and splash, the blue woollen
Jantzens, heavy with water, sagging
away from our impudent breasts?

DEATH OF A DANDY PRAT

dupped here, grey teg-
ument tight across
bones' armature, daddles

bare of stick flams and
famble cheats, the gnarly
lies, his clarty Joseph

cast aside, queer
kicks in rags. Stars burl
inward, the parched sun

swallows its
tongue, din
clouds press down

Cancer pagurus
crawls from its shell
invades him

nothing – he sinks
through the machair
into calcined turf

in time, High Springs
will claim the cool
craped wallydraigle

THE QUILT

Soon afterward, she begins to sew,
picking up the work as time and grief allow,
laying it aside when things get hard.
The stitching is tricky, the scraps irregular,
their textures uneven. This is a blue tweed
jacket her mother buttoned her into.

These squares came from a red flowered frock
found between packets of dried fruit in a wartime
food parcel. She fingers it, remembering
the first time she wore it, remembers Edward
the sweetness of that long first kiss. A fragment
of chiffon is fragile, stained by *La Rose* and violence.

She puts it aside, searches through the scrap box,
lifts out a swatch of silver lamé from a ball-dress
holds it to her waist, curtseys to the looking glass
to the tall one-eyed veteran who rescued
the wallflower and led her onto the floor. Was it
a waltz, foxtrot, quickstep, a Scottish reel?

They are all here, sewn into the quilt. She is tired
her fingers grow stiff, swollen, but now
there are only a few more patches to add.
A silk scarf, a torn flag, this handful of rose petals,
the hunted hare, Mr. Allsop's leggy Charleston,
bits from a torn wedding veil, long gloves, a shawl.

Or perhaps an unworn christening robe, his
chance-discovered affairs, snowdrops, letters
from his mistresses, a lost wedding ring.
When the quilt is finished she wraps it tightly
round the dead child then slips out into the dark
dancing again to death's beguiling tune.

HIGH FLYER

On the bedside table your cup has left a stain
which will out-stay you, for you and your new
suitcase have snapped shut and now you look
seaward, are curt, deaf to our stuttering as
the car and I make a hesitant start.

The runway squats, black as liquorice beneath
the clustering seagulls, a froth of scum scuds
before the wind. Your kiss is quick, cool, well
practised. Hands in pockets, I turn my collar up
against chill rods of stinging rain.

The plane lifts up on fine white wings of spray.
My sweet high-flyer, a blue sky holds you now,
way above our clouds; you've become no more
than a silver fleck, a mote held safe in the warm
eye of another, distant sun.

Back home, your wet footsteps are still leaving
but for a night or two more the bed and I will share
what's left of you: traces of diesel, a small depression,
Marlboro ash. Safe in our creased sheets I'll not hear
as the sea and my future crash against the door.

POVERTY PIG

Dusk over Jasper County and here
he comes, old Dasypus, nocturnal
plodder, snuffling past us on the road
toward Hampton. Small Armoured
One, they've called him, Azotochtli,
Hoover Hog but names do not
concern him. Unhurried, stopping
only to sniff the air or forage verges
with snout and claws, stuffing in
grubs, beetles, tubers, the occasional
frog, with just a flick of his tongue.
The journey's been a long one, from
the rainforests, across the Isthmus,
the Rio Grande, Texas, Florida, over
swamps, scrublands and prairies,
leaving a trail of fusty burrows.
Now he heads on up for Kentucky,
Nebraska, Illinois and look, he can put
on a turn of speed if needed, has
a trick of jumping three or four
feet high when trouble threaten. At
such times it's a toss-up who will come
off worse, Dasypus novemcinctus
or Homo Sapiens, all those good 'ol
boys hollering after him in battered
pickup trucks and rusty Chevys.

A LATE NIGHT AT YOSHI'S

Freight trains mourn past us as we cross Jack London Square,
making our way to Yoshi's on Embarcadero West. By ten it's
hot and crowded, but you, you're so cool. In that cream jacket,
Italian shirt, chinos and favourite pair of tasseled loafers,
you shimmer in the gloom. The waitresses flit round,
point their sharp breasts, toss their hair sweetly, ignore me.

You say the menu is a poem, read it lovingly, caress each word
before at last you choose Kamo Kushiyaki, maple-leaf duck
in tamari balsamic, while I, you insist, must try the delicate
Kona Kampuchea, a tartare of Asian pear, wasabi flower, yuzu
and cucumber, plus, for both of us, their special Tamanishiki rice.

By now I'm thinking it will take something more than all of this
to get me through the night, something much stronger than
the suggested glass of iced ginger-peach darjeeling. You order
the house white, sniffing, lips pursed, twirling the glass, holding it
up to the light, a performance which drives me to sink my way
down the list of twenty recommended crisp, round, fragrant sakes.

It's eleven before the show begins. Rocket leads blind Deedles
to the Concert Grand. Outrageous, bawdy, she attacks the keys.
It don't mean a thing if it ain't got that swing, she belts out, then
swoops her way through all the hits she made with Stan Getz
Ray Charles, Maynard Ferguson and B.B. King.

Me, I'm more of a Captain Beefheart fan, but then she ends
with 'September in the Rain', first recorded at the Holiday Inn,
Tacoma, when she was only ten and sings now for her dead
mother, weeping as the audience weeps with her.

I weep too, but blame my tears more on you, the waitresses,
those bloody loafers and probably the sake. *Some other time*,
I think, *Sure, Deedles, so damned right, some other time.*

THE FRIG-PIG

Here's a tight one, cullies,
here's a woolly-crown, a right
Sir Quibble-Queere, tricked out
in caster and farting-crackers,
flashing his cod-fambles, fop-
mincing down Feather-bed lane,
Tip me a Gage of fogus,
yer honour, I says,
dandles outstretched.
Away with you, you bran-
faced brim, says he
and pikes off, the broad-
bound badge-cove,
glim in hand, marvellous eager
to yam on quacking-cheats
at some Mumpers Hall
with every gill-flurt, foyst,
wet-quaker and dilly-mop
in town. It won't fadge
to have him worm'd here
with yelpers on the prowl
but I gives a whindle, draws
a check'd wiper off him
and toutes his munns,
May the Flap-dragon get yer,
yer prigging Frig-pig, I calls
after him, and wishes him
well-frummagemmed
before dark's through.

BRINDLE REVISITED

The Helm wind howls down Duxon Hill,
weeds lengthen in the cobbled yard,
the lime trees on the lawn are gone,
stained-glass lies scattered on the path.

The dove-house timbers rot away
rainwater pools the cattle-trough,
the governess-cart has shed its wheels,
toads squat behind a pile of turf.

The stable walls run green with mould,
a row of mildewed bridles hang
abandoned in the harness room,
the rat-runs in the barn fall in.

The parqueted drawing-room is bare
of Bechstein grand and rust-red rug,
the library grate is ash-filled, cold,
the Eagle range bakes no more bread.

Slate shelves hold neither cakes nor cream.
and now where eight of us once played
no-one spurs Jack, the rocking horse,
across the silent nursery.

Yet from the windows, looking north,
still Cumberland's grey mountains loom
still, to the west, a snail-trail sea,
still, to the east, the wild Helm wind –

and to the south, on Duxon Hill
the lapwings call and circle still.

AND

and then the platform's empty
and the train's pulling out
and she tries to run alongside
and bang on the windows
and her legs won't move
and the sound comes on
and someone is singing *Que reste-t-il de tout cela*
and a sign says *Sortie*
and she knows it's time to leave
and she still has his book
and the pages are uncut
and his words are unread
and the question is…
and she already knows the answer
and that is now the end, she thinks
and then the strange thing happens
and a voice says *write your own*
and that is her beginning
and a luna moth settles on her wrist
and spreads its luminous green wings.

BALLYWHEREVER

gulls, fish scales on sun-sharp knives.

Carmel, she says, Carmel did you hear I lost me husband

ah God, Kathy isn't there always something?

swallows are slicing up the sky between them

try a little cream with the carrageen jelly now?

they were halfway up Narrow Street then they saw the pig

goldfinches at the feeder blue tits nest in the roof's corrugations

they say Siobhan had a nasty mishap last Friday

were your courgettes nice didn't I win 1st prize with them

and had them for me dinner afterward

he called her an ill-bred slut said no decent man could live with her

so I told her the man's an eejit will I put the kettle on?

I swear to God, Mhairi she never ate a banana again

cow-parsley ransoms bluebells cranesbills lady's mantle forget-me-nots

it's misty over there right enough tarragon might go better with that

the moon has eaten the lilacs

DR STAGBANT REFLECTS

Two years since she left; once again
it is the time of elderflower and hawthorn.

Twenty four months gone by; once
more it is the time of the soft white roses

which have shaken themselves free
and now weep softly on the grass

but may I draw your attention to
the absurd fragility of these harebells

and how they droop their heads
beneath the urgent weight of bees?

Indeed, one has to question
how such stems support them.

Consider, too, how the sun at noon
has turned the purple bramble tips

translucent, just there, where blades
of jade push between that scumble

of dead leaves. I would like to record
all this, and that I put it down to love.

DR STAGBANT TALKS OF ROSES

Let us walk in the garden for a while,
I would like to show you to my roses,
as that rogue Sheridan would have it.

Meet my dear friends: see, here
is General Jaqueminot, a fine fellow,
is he not? Though perhaps a little florid

and let me present you to Louise Odier,
a pretty thing despite that unfortunate
last name. Have a mind to those loose

paving stones: the terrace is aging, as
alas, am I. Look, Cardinal de Richelieu,
is nodding to the Empereur du Maroc

and you will have noted, will you not,
how these soft and subtle shades of purple,
mauve and lilac are my preference,

how they suit my pensive moods,
my melancholy humeurs in these lone
years of mourning? Tell me now,

do you recall those lines of Ronsard,
written for Cassandre. Let me see, how
do they go? Something like this, no?

Mignonne, allons voir si la rose
Qui ce matin avoit desclose
Sa robe de pourpre au Soleil…

etcetera, etcetera. Some scholars have it
that the dress is scarlet, but most surely
they are wrong, would you not agree?

No, no, Ronsard must have had in mind
a rose like this one, Daphne, my latest
acquisition, a gallica, her silken petals

tumbled in most charming disarray.
Let me pluck one for you – ah, how
both of you do scent the evening air.

CHARMEUSE

It's the way it runs through his fingers, fluid
jet; the liquefaction, gleam, glister, glisten,
slink and sheen of it. At first he buys them for her,
always black, then steals them back, one at a time,
holds them to his face, rubs them against his skin.
The compulsion strengthens, he ravages washing
lines, marauds the bedrooms of his neighbour's
wives, preferring moonlit nights with that risk
of discovery, the lures of paraphilia accelerating
with danger. Lighted windows seduce him; women
dress and undress, their shadow-play turns him on.
The collection grows; its sinuous folds embrace
his hips, groin and thighs, arousing him. In time, some
pieces fade; he researches The Restoration of Black Silk.
Boil logwood, immerse garment, simmer; take out, put
to the dye a little blue vitriol or green coperas. Now
replace garment, simmer again. Or use a decoction
of fig-leaves. He chooses a decoction of fig leaves,
soaks and stirs. The tenebrous gloss returns.

RED CHIFFON

If I could reclaim her it would be this way

she is wearing the red chiffon it clings to her

frothing out below her knees into frills and ruffles

a slender fish a mermaid a fire-angel a tongue of flame

Quick, quick, my little stick carry me over the stream

when the story of Ezmond and the witch is finished

she closes the Blue Fairy Book adds a last coal to the grate

sends the shadows into a brief retreat

God Bless,

with her thumb she draws a cross

upon my forehead

I can't bear her beauty the pity of her violet scent

the hole that's left when she leaves the room

or the shadows which come crowding back

if it wasn't for the firelight I would choke

on the emptiness

KEEPING TIME

there's an edgy scent of winter in the air, of
chrysanthemums, azaleas, wood smoke, frost

music flows through the drawing room
and laps the windows at the further side

before the others come, my father takes my hand
then we're away, swept up by the music's swell

circling across the chevronned parquet floor
his arm firm round my waist as I lean back, safe

for a while, the music thrumming in my head
one-two-three, one-two-three, one-two-three

as I try to get it right, for these are the good times
when he's happy, foot-sure, handsome in his tails

humming all the bits he can't quite remember
the blue Danube flows, pom pom, pom pom

and I'm feeling grown-up in black moiré taffeta
a sister's hand-me-down, much too old for me

while by the old gramophone, a four-foot high
monolith of mahogany, frayed silk and brass

my mother stands, smiling her sad smile
cranking the crooked handle as we waltz past

the river eddying round us, spinning us on
and on until I'm dizzy – reverse, advance, reverse.

IN AND OUT OF THE KITCHEN

Hilda and Nancy are singing: *Red sails*
in the sunset, they sing, *red sails on the sea…*
and the silent child who sits there
beneath the long scrubbed table
floats out on the dog's plaid cushion
into a sky as red as the tomatoes
Hilda and Nancy are bottling, while
a man on the wireless says
that no such undertaking has been
received, and Hilda and Nancy
stop singing. *That's it, then,* says
Hilda, and *We'll be for it*, says Nancy,
but the child on the cushion boat sails
on, far away, up over the oak woods,
Livsey's field of shorthorns, high
over old Miss Gatty's house,
Quakerbrook Lane, The Boar's Head
and Millstone farm. When she gets back
there'll be hot milk, iced biscuits, a long
blacked-out night and skies burning
redder than she could ever imagine.

NIGHT SHIFT, BURNHAM DEEPDALE

The Norfolk night is damson, still,
only the scratching
of your intermittent breath
frets at the silence.

Hours elide, shifts change, the doctor
shakes her head, smiles, says
you should have gone a month ago
but now all bets are off.

Stay-at-home sister, these past weeks
you have slipped free
from the iron-bars of the bed
to go traveling at last

but the journey's not been easy.
Why, you whispered, did I leave you
in the desert without water,
on a mountain without food?

I lift back a strand of hair,
swab your lips, your blind eyes,
change sheets, replace the rosary
in your restless fingers.

THE PRIVY, EASINGWOLD

Seventy-one years ago, Father,
Mother and I staying at an icy Bed
and Breakfast by a frozen stream
in this blacked-out Yorkshire village.
I'm eight, running through the dark
with chattering teeth and tin lantern
to the whitewashed WC, its wooden
seat still warm from someone here
before. Scraps of torn newspaper
hang from a nail, there's a smell
of soot and mould, something rots
beneath a pile of rusting leaves,
moths brush my face, spiders lurk
but despite all this I like it here,
sitting with the door propped open
by a brick, can see and name the stars,
planets, galaxies and constellations
shown me by my father, hear him
say *Look, love, there's Cassiopeia,*
Orion's Belt, Venus, the Little Bear –
inside the house, my mother tries
out 'Für Elise' on the upright piano's
yellow keys and suddenly I'm happy
to be alone, drifting away from them
both for the first time, held safe
in this great starriness of space.

STUCK IN OUAGADOUGOU WITH YOU

(Haibun)

In Ecuador it was Edou. We made love on deserted beaches, I traced his body's outline in the sand, tasted his salt flecked skin that still held memories of the wrecked slave ship. He was my first, taught me everything, made me taste *tronquito*, that fiery bull's-penis soup, spoon-fed me with Eugenia ice cream, dripping it into my pleading mouth Oh, that ice cream, those ripe sour-sweet Eugenia fruits, that brief sweet sour romance. But now, dear God, where am I? Stuck here, with you, in Ouagadougou.

I played away with Esteban in Extramadura. What that boy did not know and could not do wasn't worth a deep-fried eggplant. Sometimes we made it a threesome with his teenage brother in the dark forests of the *dehesia's* oak trees. I knew things to be done with a string of pearls but the memory of that kid's ingenuity with a handful of acorns makes me tremble. After long, entangled siestas the boys would still be up for it, climbing the wardrobe to launch themselves with wild *Olés* into brave attempts at the *Sauté de Tigré*, but now, dear God, where am I? Stuck here, with *you*, in Ouagadougou.

Last week in Enniskean I was back in the arms of Eamonn, my dear, my darling, my sweet bit of rough from County Cork; a great big broth of a boy who was handy and into a bit of poaching, Gubbeen bacon, a glass or three of Paddy's and the *craic*. How I loved him, took him where he'd never been, showed him things he'd ever even thought of. I kept it simple, fed him with eggy bread and Eccles cakes, sated him with mouth and hands and elderberry wine, promised to return. But now, dear God, where am I? Because of a lousy volcano, stuck here with you in Ouagadougou.

The days were sweet, I drank the wine,
I ate the meat, each lovely boy my reckless
treat, but now, dear God I'm stuck
with you in sodding Ouagadougou.

TYING HIS FEET

From that first time, down by the river,
when he took me by surprise and
I was swept up in a storm of feathers,
dissolving under the ruthless beat of wings,
I persuaded myself it was useless to struggle
for there was no gentleness till afterwards
but then such tenderness, such enfolding,
such sinuous caresses, the special smell of him,
weed and water and something else
I couldn't quite place, something cloacal perhaps,
whatever, it sent me wild, I couldn't help myself,
couldn't get enough of him. We'd meet
most afternoons, safe in our green tent
of willow, I never tired of it. Of course
things couldn't last. He grew jealous,
demanding, began following me home,
loitering round the house, peering in
at windows. My husband noticed web-prints
on the path, swansdown in the bed, in my hair,
wondered how it got there, where it came from.
This had to stop; next day, as Swan lay languorous,
I twisted twine round his beak, his wings,
his poor black feet, and, before he knew it,
had him bundled into the back seat
of the old Humber, the glass screen between us.
For miles he struggled, beaked against it,
but then gave in, quietened, seemed resigned.
I kissed him once, twice, delivered him
to the RSPB, told them how I'd found him
by the road, and what some people would do
to a helpless bird was unbelievable. The drive home
was lonely. I sang old songs but it didn't help.
Next day my husband sold the car, said
there was a smell that turned his stomach, that
the indicators were jammed and anyway, the big-end
was about to go. On cold nights I hear wings.